Mastery | The
of
People

Every man who knows how to read has it in his power to magnify himself, to multiply the ways in which he exists, to make his life full, significant and interesting.
—ALDOUS HUXLEY

THE

MASTERY

OF

PEOPLE

AUREN URIS

Prentice-Hall, Inc., Englewood Cliffs, N.J.

Library of Congress Catalog Card Number: 64–16433

Fourth printing . . . . .April, 1966

56003—B&P

table of contents

Part I

Join and Win
the Human Race

chapter 1

You want things out of life—
the good things. You want the
warmth of deep and abiding
friendship; pleasant relations
with your neighbors; the respect—yes, and admiration—of
the people you work with; the
approval and love of your
family.

To have these things
means to achieve the best life
has to offer. The person who
succeeds in winning his way
to these goals has converted
his life from mediocrity and
failure to outstanding success.

Yet few people ever come
anywhere near accomplishing
the ends they so earnestly
desire. They go through life,
day to day, with little to
show but frustration, disappointment, and eventually the
feeling that their lack of
achievement is due to lack of
ability. In the bitter secret
moments of self-confrontation
that we all have, one time or
another, they admit to themselves, "I guess I just don't
have what it takes."

Nonsense! To me, this ad-

the real
secret of
mastery
over others

3

mission of failure is not only a stupid, self-deceiving lie, but an affront, a denial of the almost unlimited potential with which nature has endowed every one of us.

Yet once one admits defeat all effort for winning the victory of life usually ceases. Then the personal enemy that lies in wait for all of us appears out of hiding, and takes over. The enemy? The deadly enervator, the vampire that sucks us dry of ambition, hope and our chance for success—Apathy!

Look about you at life's failures, the men and women at jobs that hold little satisfaction and even less pay check. Recall the people in your community who hover in the background while the leaders create the ideas and drive that make your town a lively and progressive entity. It is apathy that keeps them back, that binds them as tightly as iron chains, and renders them impotent.

Lord knows, the victims of apathy deserve our pity more than blame. Life *can be* cruel and ruthless. Probe the past of a confirmed failure, and you almost always find defeat: they were unable to land the "one good job," or "get that one break" that, they say, would have put them on top.

But dig deeper than these explanations—and I have, with scores of career-blighted individuals—and you find a striking uniformity of attitude:

"I don't know how to go about being successful."

"I don't know where to start, what direction to move. . . ."

The next few paragraphs and pages of this book contain a positive answer to these statements. The answer is one that has brought wealth, status, satisfaction to hundreds of people—and can do the same for you! There is nothing mysterious about the method. On the contrary, it is the simplest thing in the world to understand, and easy to apply. Why, then, haven't the hundreds who were successful been thousands, even tens of thousands?

I said the idea *can* make you successful, bring you the things in life that enrich it, and make it a joy and a satisfaction.

Will it? That depends on whether you are able to do the one thing that foils so many people. Slay the slimy dragon, Apathy, and just as sure as the sun rises, your progress toward your objectives will amaze you.

There is another hazard that keeps individuals from the achievement they so sincerely desire. Those who have not succumbed to the monster, Apathy, wear themselves out rushing down blind alleys, applying their energies to circular paths that will take them to no worthwhile destination, and leave them, finally, back near their starting point.

If you want a clue to the success secret about to be told to you, turn to the very first paragraph in this chapter. Note the elements in our various aspirations for success. Friends, neighbors, those we work with, family, were mentioned.

Yes, *people* are the common denominator. People hold the key to the goals we want to achieve. Do you have any doubts? Then let the experience of others underscore the validity of this fact.

• *The Straight Road to Success.* "If there is a single universal key to success, it lies in the ability to command the cooperation of people," says Irving I. Stone, president of the American Greetings Corporation, one of the country's largest greeting card firms. Stone is his own best example. In 1934, he was one of the firm's two employees. Now, three decades later, he is head of the company of 4000 employees in 12 different plants.

Many voices have uttered the same thought, in every language and in every era. But in our time, the mastery of people has taken on a new importance. More and more, we've become aware that what we do, what we become, what we accomplish in our lives, depends on how well we can influence the thoughts and actions of our friends and neighbors, our subordinates and colleagues at work.

Recently, a large Eastern university conducted a survey covering 2000 graduates. The purpose of the study was to find out who had succeeded and who had failed after ten years, and the reasons why. It was found that *the major reason for failure to get ahead was inability to get along with people.*

• *The Power of People Management.* Two cases, one on a job, one in the club life of a community, show what's involved:

Peter Fellers has recently been promoted from clerk to head of the mailroom of a Wall Street brokerage house. Whether or not he makes a go of his new job depends on how he succeeds in getting the obedience and cooperation of his group, who just yesterday were his co-workers.

Henry Darrin helped form a boat club that has set up quarters on the Connecticut River, near Hadlyme. To his dismay, he sees a clique forming that threatens to defeat the original aims of the group, and convert it into a social Saturday-night-party affair. Whether or not he'll be able to save the situation depends on how well he can persuade other group members to his point of view.

John Craig, manufacturing executive of Westinghouse, expressed the pre-eminence of human relations skill in these words: "No matter how much work a man can do, no matter how engaging his personality may be, he will not advance if he cannot work through others."

Harry Resnick, president of Channelmaster Corporation, an electronics firm, has emphasized the power of people management even more pointedly: "Even if you can't drive a nail or a bulldozer, if the one thing you can do is manage people, your future is assured."

Despite the assertions of qualified men such as Stone, Craig and Resnick, a core of disbelief still lingers. We find it difficult to accept the fact that the ability to master people, which is, after all, an intangible, can yield material benefits.

The doubt here is akin to that of the elderly but practical-minded grandmother who asked her college grandson to explain Einstein's Theory of Relativity. The young man strove manfully to put the idea in laymen's language. The old lady nodded as his explanation progressed. But when he had finished, her comment was, "Do you mean to tell me that Einstein made a living from nonsense like that?"

But yes, you *can* capitalize in many ways, *including cold cash*, on your mastery of people. The steel magnate, Andrew Carnegie, not one to throw his money away carelessly, paid Charles M. Schwab a million dollars a year to run the Carnegie Steel Company. Schwab himself explained why:

"I consider my ability to arouse enthusiasm among the men," said Schwab, "the greatest asset I possess."

• *Twin Paths to Failure.* Actually, the crucial importance of being able to manage people has finally been accepted by most people. And yet, despite positive efforts, many really capable individuals get nowhere. The reason? They make fumbling attempts based on naive and ineffectual ideas. Here are two common approaches, both doomed to failure:

. . . *the get-sweet ploy.* "I'll make them like me, then they'll do what I want," thinks the young college boy, put in charge of a teenage group at a summer camp. But the disciplinary problems become worse than ever.

. . . *the get-tough gambit.* "I'll show 'em who's boss," storms the junior executive, and in the process of throwing his weight around, he kills the last shred of hope for getting any cooperation at all from his people.

• *Take the Arrow-Straight Road to Achievement.* Fortunately, there is a road to mastery of people that works. The method has been time-tested, proved successful again and again. Learning a single basic principle can put you way ahead of the game. This approach can make easy for you relationships with people that may have been impossible before. It can win for you the mastery of others that is intimately bound up with advancement and satisfaction in every aspect of your life, at home and on the job.

Don't get the wrong idea. It isn't easy to master people. If it were, everybody could do it, and there would be no need for you to be concerned, or for me to write this book. No, it isn't easy—*but it can be made easy!*

A single idea, a principle of action, can set you light years ahead in your ability to influence people. A man named Ed Adams shows you the way.

• *The Tool Concept.* There's a carpenter in my town named Ed Adams. If it's woodwork you want, Ed's your man. He can put together anything from a perfectly joined shelf to a sturdy cottage. One thing about Ed, he never works with his bare hands. Whether he's building a shelf or a house, he needs and uses tools. Armed with hammer, saw, chisel, square, Ed can work wonders. Without tools, Ed's helpless.

Ed's example gives us an important clue to accomplishment, to our desire for success. He shows us that in tackling *any* job—whether it's building a cabinet or a career—tools make the crucial difference! Too often, we attempt to tackle life's tasks and problems barehanded. *We try to meet our challenges, solve our problems, make our way in the world of people without the benefit of tools we're all endowed with but seldom put to work.*

Ed Adams couldn't put two sticks together without tools. Yet many people attempt to accomplish the infinitely more complex job of mastering people, and thereby building successful lives and careers, without the help of nature's tools. We want to win better jobs, more worthwhile careers, the respect and regard of others. And most people go about it in a naive, barehanded way that's guaranteed to fail!

There's an infinitely better alternative than the empty-handed approach to the mastery of people. It's demonstrated by the carpenter, the draftsman, the sculptor, the engineer, the business executive, all the

professional users of tools in our society. All successful professionals
have one thing in common. They are masters of the implements of
their craft. Without tools, they are ineffectual, doomed to waste energy
and effort, and eventually to fail. With tools, they are masters of the
most complex tasks and problems.

By following the better way, by using the biological, psychological
and social tools for working with people that nature has endowed you
with, you multiply your chances for success tenfold. It's as simple as
A B C. You learn:

A. To be aware of your personal tools;
B. To sharpen them;
C. To use them *knowingly*, to win success on the job and in your
   personal life through the control, the domination, the mastery
   of people.

The means for scoring successes in our relations with others are our
human relations skills. Every one of us possesses a rich natural endow-
ment of these supremely valuable tools, but only one in a hundred puts
them to work. Most people leave their tools for managing people on
the shelf, to rust and deteriorate from lack of use. You needn't be
among their number. You become a supreme craftsman of people by
learning to develop and use your human relations skills, the tools of the
accomplished master of people.

From time to time we observe an outstandingly successful individual
—one who has won his way to the economic or social heights. And we
wonder, "How did he do it?" Be sure of one thing. It wasn't done with
the empty-handed approach. The successful person uses tools, the
weapons of success we'll be describing and showing you how to use in
the pages ahead.

• *Two Successful Tool Users.* The tools for fashioning your success
are already at hand, in your possession. But most of us are unaware of
them, partly because they come in such a great variety of shapes and
sizes. Just consider:

R. J. Thomas is a highly successful sales manager. "Knowing how
to motivate people is my strongest selling tool," he confides. "Too often
people listen with indifference. I have learned to make them listen and
to act. And my skill at motivating others has helped me sell millions of
dollars worth of business."

Motivating people to take action, a *tool?* Yes, one of the most effective there is, for managing people. It's covered in Chapter 16.

Jerry Frankland is known as a master marketer. He's consulted by big companies who want to know how to go about putting across their products. "My biggest skill," explains Jerry, "is my ability to read people's minds, detect their feelings and reactions. It helps me assess what they're likely to do in a given situation, tells me what the 'mood of the day' is."

Ability to read people's minds a *tool*? Yes, it can change an unaware fumbler into an alert accomplisher. Chapter 6 tells you all about this unusual but effective implement for greater personal effectiveness. Go through the Table of Contents to see the array of human relations tools you have available to win the things you want.

• *The Secret of Man's Power.* Scientists who study the development of man from his early cave man days to the present, when he stands astride the spaceways like a demigod, attribute his miraculous advance to his mastery of tools. Dr. Nehemiah Jordan of the Rand Corporation puts it quite matter of factly, "A tool extends man's ability both sensory and material . . . tools have, since their inception as eoliths, served to make a difficult job easier and an impossible job possible."

"Man is a tool-using animal . . . without tools he is nothing, with tools he is all," said Thomas Carlyle, the great Scottish essayist.

• *Your Tool Kit for Accomplishment.* People can scale the heights of success by using such implements as persuasiveness, analytical skill, creativity, leadership ability. Those that can transform your life are certainly included in this list—and in the chapters ahead.

Once you become aware of the implements you have at your beck and call, life will suddenly seem full of unexplored opportunities:

. . . important human relations problems will no longer seem insurmountable. On the contrary, new solutions will appear to eliminate old stumbling blocks, now that you have powerful weapons at your command. People who may have been your enemies, or competitors, can be cut to size. People on whom your progress depends, your boss, for example, can be made to take positive action on your behalf.

. . . life's challenges will no longer seem formidable. On the contrary, your goals of today will be your accomplishments of tomorrow, with the new command of people your personal skills give you. You'll get greater cooperation, people will back you up, go all out to help, because now, for the first time, you know how to motivate them.

Your personal skills, wielded with understanding and precision will give you the feeling of power—that is, self-confidence. And you will win the *reward* of power, that is, *success*.

Obviously not everyone needs the same tools. In some situations, for example, it will be your ability to read people's minds, to understand what they think and still more important, what they *feel* that can tip the scales in your favor. In another situation it may be your skill at getting a person to level with you, tell you the truth about a situation.

This ability to choose the right tool, to make use of the appropriate implement in a given situation, is what distinguishes the master golfer from the duffer, the man who accomplishes from the one who merely "wishes he could," the master of people from the failure. In the pages ahead you will find the guidance you need to make this critical selection of the right tool for the job.

▶ Recap ◀

To help you pin down the essentials of this chapter:

The tool we've been talking about: The Tool Concept, *itself a tool,* is a key to understanding that the mastery of people need not be undertaken "barehanded." You are naturally endowed with tools that help you master people—those on whom your aspirations and satisfactions depend.

How and when to use it: You apply the Tool Concept to every human relations problem. Consider your problem, and ask, "What tool would it take to guarantee success?" Whether it's the ability to persuade, or to read people's minds, you're almost sure to find it listed in the Table of Contents of this book.

How to develop it: Develop your ability to wield the Tool Concept by applying it to real problems. For example, Al Heffler, of White Bear Lake, Minnesota, told me: "I wanted my neighbor to sell me a strip of land that adjoined mine, and I'd been unsuccessful. Finally, I applied your Tool Concept, asked, 'What tool do I need to get him to go along?' Persuasion was the answer. I followed your advice in Chapter 11—and it worked!"

chapter 2

"I guess I must have the biggest inferiority complex this side of the Mississippi."

"I can't get people to accept my leadership. . . ."

"People frighten me. . . ."

In my files I have dozens of statements like these from individuals who, with good reason, feel they haven't made the grade.

The sad fact is, at the heart of this type of inadequacy is a single flaw, a failure in *attitude toward people*.

This chapter will help you untangle some ideas and feelings about people *in general* that often are confused in our minds. As a result of this confusion, trouble with people *in particular* is unavoidable. Once this tangle is unkinked for you, problems of dealing with colleagues, subordinates, friends or acquaintances that may have haunted you before will vanish, and the impossible in human relationships will become easy. You will find your attitude toward people a tremendous asset, instead of a lethal liability.

**get acquainted
with the
human race
— and shake
a hidden fear**

11

"To work wood, know wood"

Chaim Gross is one of our greatest contemporary sculptors. I had the honor and privilege of briefly studying with this outstanding artist. Gross is largely responsible for reviving the nearly vanished art of wood carving. His intimate knowledge of wood makes possible his impressive works in this medium.

Gross used to say to his students, "If you're going to work in wood, you must know wood."

In the same way it can be said: "If you're going to work with people, you must know people."

Phil Hill, of California, winner of the 1962 Le Mans 24-Hour Race, attributes his victory largely to his knowledge of the terrain of the grueling contest. He had gone over the tricky French roadways many times in preparation for the race.

To be a master in any field, you must know the lay of the land, be familiar with the territory in which you are to operate. Accordingly, as mentioned previously, to master people, *you must know people.*

Now, you may think that, aside from the question of whether or not it's easy to do, the meaning of the phrase *know people* is crystal clear. But it's precisely because of this common misconception that a large percentage of would-be masters and managers of people fall by the wayside. That simple imperative, *Know people,* isn't as simple as it seems. Actually, there's a built-in hazard, an obstacle that trips up many simply because it's hidden!

Examine those two words, *know people.* Whom do we mean when we say *people?* Do we mean those with whom we come in contact? Do we mean every one of the nearly three billion souls that inhabit the earth? The word *people* can cover both these groups, and dozens more. Obviously, there's a need for clarification.

Clearing up the semantic confusion

Let's get straight on this important point. The word *people* will be used in this chapter to mean people in general, the human race, mankind. And don't for one moment think this is an exercise in semantic hairsplitting. *Far from it.* The distinction is made, not to create an unnecessary complication, but to clarify vital differences. The word *people* can be taken to mean:

1. People in general, for example, those that make up the human race, or your community.

2. Specific people, those with whom you come in contact, and on whom your human relations tools must be wielded on the job and off.

I repeat, in this chapter, we're interested in talking about people in the first sense, that is, people in general.

It's important to be clear on these different meanings of the word *people* because your feelings and relationships may vary widely with each.

For example, it's possible—and not illogical—for a person to hate *people* (meaning people in general) but to like people (individuals, like Tom, Dick, and Harry).

The importance of attitude

When you deal with people, the question of attitude is crucial. For example, in selling, the importance of attitude is clearly understood. Victor I. Bumagin, who directs sales for the Collier-Macmillan Library Division, says, "One of the chief differences between a top salesman and a mediocre one is *attitude.* The top man approaches people with an open, confident, self-assured manner. The less successful man has a kind of fragmented attitude, made up of one-third hope, one-third fear, and one-third self doubt."

When I was a production foreman in the Plastics Division of the Celanese Corporation of America, a young fellow-foreman of mine whose real name I won't mention, faced a serious morale problem. In Joe's punch press department worked many men of middle-European origin. Joe rode these employees unmercifully, was constantly breathing down their necks. "You can't trust those foreigners," he confided to me bitterly. Morale—and production—in his department was the lowest in the company.

Notice how his failure was caused by his attitude? His destructive behavior followed naturally from his basic feeling of suspicion and distrust towards people.

Accept it as an unvarying rule: *the person who has trouble dealing with people has basic attitudes that are getting in his way.*

Now let's get on with the aspect of this subject that's really important to both of us, namely, *your* attitude toward people in general.

What's your opinion of the human race?

Let's start by talking about *people* as a unique race, the most fascinating beings on Earth, and as far as we know right now, on any other planet.

With due modesty, we must admit we're a unique group.

How can we help but regard with amazement a race that produces an Einstein and a Hitler, a Charlemagne and a Capone, martyrs and murderers, heroes and cowards, women who give up their lives rather than lose their honor, and women who sell their souls for a few trinkets.

Yes, we're a great, glorious, puzzling, bewildering, fascinating *people*. And getting right to the point—what's your attitude towards your baffling fellow humans?

Rid yourself of a secret fear

Speak of Man with a capital M, of *people* in general, and an unconscious reaction takes place in most of us. Basically, it's one of awe. Many poets have expressed this feeling of respect and wonder. For example, Shakespeare wrote:

What a piece of work is man! How noble in reason! How infinite in faculties! In form and moving, how express and admirable! In action, how like an angel! In apprehension, how like a god!

Most of us share with Shakespeare a deep awe of the Being, Man. And it's this feeling that prevents many of us from developing the very dominance we seek! How can we hope to influence and control when we're hindered by feelings towards people that range from wonder to dread?

Isn't it true that now, at this very moment, you find yourself cowed, intimidated by the scope of your topic? Are you overwhelmed by Man spelled with a capital M? Good! That's the very feeling that must be brought out into the open. It's because this feeling of awe towards our fellow man remains *hidden, repressed,* that so many fail in the conquest of the individuals on whom our mastery depends.

Why a personnel assistant
never got any further

I've talked to many men and women about obstacles that arise because of their feelings towards people in general. One man, an assistant personnel officer in a Chicago bank told me, "You have to have a lot of ego to tell other people what to do. I could never muster enough self-confidence to control people. That's why I've been an assistant here for ten years—and I'll never advance any further."

In the interview that followed, this man was able to identify for the first time what it was that held him back: "I guess I've always been afraid of people. . . ."

He had finally put his finger on his weakness. People *in general* had him buffaloed. Practically all his adult life he had been dealing not with *individuals,* but with *people en masse!* He never saw himself in a one-to-one relationship with a person, but in conflict with the whole human race! If he were dealing with one of the bank tellers, he'd worry about the effect of their conversation on the other tellers. What might "others" think? If he were reprimanding a secretary for lateness, his efforts would be thrown off by concern about what others would think —and by *others* he meant everybody from his boss to the guard up front!

Get rid of the feeling that "others" are watching you, learn to focus on the people, the only people, who matter—*those you're dealing with at the moment.*

During the Korean War, a G.I. newly arrived at the front huddled in a blue funk, frozen at the thought of the rampaging Chinese hordes he had to face.

"Ease up," a kindly veteran told him. "You don't have to fight them all, only the ones that come up over that hill."

By freeing yourself from the hidden fears about *people in general,* by airing self-doubt based on fear of man in the mass, you can reach new heights of self-confidence, reassure yourself on your ability to control people as *individuals.* As good old Casey Stengel used to say when he was on top, "We play 'em one at a time."

With this one obstacle out of the way, with the false notion eliminated that you must pit yourself against *people* to master people, you can go on with heightened assurance of success.

How do you really feel about people?

Here's your chance to see how you really feel about people. It's an important piece of self-knowledge because *your attitude towards people is a tool in your management of people.* The brief self-test below will help you determine just how you do regard your fellow man. Use the chart below as follows:

Read the paired statements as they are grouped below. Then put a mark at the point on the line that best represents your attitude. Take the first for example: if you feel *people* are completely nasty beings, check the point nearest that statement, zero. If your feelings are half-way between the two statements, then put your mark at the midpoint, and so on. Proceed in the same way for the next two.

"Scratch below surface and you find *people* are nasty, selfish, grasping."	0 2 4 6 8 (10)	"Essentially *people* are kind, generous, trustworthy."
"I prefer being alone to being with others. *People* are tiresome and boring."	0 2 4 6 8 10	"I enjoy the company of others, prefer socializing to almost any other type of entertainment."
"As far as *people* are concerned, it's a dog-eat-dog world."	0 2 4 6 (8) 10	"*People* are friendly, willing to help their fellow man. Many people have helped me in my life."

After you've rated yourself on each line, connect the points. This is the personal "profile" of your attitude toward *people.* We'll tell you what your profile means, shortly. First, here's what the profile reveals in general.

Three faces of evil

The three-line test above grows out of the three basic negative feelings that individuals have towards their fellow man. One can *hate* them, *fear* them, or *ignore* them. These three attitudes are not sharp and distinct. Often they overlap one another, but surely in your own experience you've seen these basic attitudes:

. . . "I hate *people*." A young girl of 17 uttered this denunciation on coming home from a dance where not a single boy had asked her out on the dance floor. One can easily dismiss the bitterness of the moment, but to many who feel themselves rejected, unloved, unwanted, this hatred of their fellow man can be an abiding sentiment. There is even a special word for the mankind hater: misanthrope. In everyday life a more common phrase usually fits. We say, "He's the meanest man in town."

. . . "my son is extremely shy," a mother says of a young man of 20, who is attempting to earn his living as a self-employed cartoonist. He tries to conduct his business by mail, to avoid the tensions and strain that people create for him.

That anti-people feeling

What's the young cartoonist's problem? People frighten him. He feels uncomfortable in the company of others. Psychologists tell us there are various explanations for this feeling. For example, one possibility is that the individual feels threatened, he somehow feels that people will insult him, humiliate him, even harm him physically. Obviously this is a neurotic, illogical fear, but to the person who suffers it, it's all too real. Even the "normal" person may be touched by this anti-*people* feeling. But then it shows itself merely as a shyness or diffidence in the presence of others.

. . . "I have as little to do with people as possible." The man who said that withdraws from the human race because he has difficulty establishing contact with his fellow human beings.

One way psychologists have of explaining this person's problem is to say, "He can't relate to others." This individual doesn't make friends easily. Somehow, even when he does have friends, the relationships tend to be clouded by quarrels and misunderstandings.

The three attitudes we've been talking about have one thing in common. They are absolutely destructive to any attempt to get along with, manage or master people. The reason is obvious. One cannot deal effectively with individuals where hate, fear, or lack of feeling exists.

Now let's turn to your profile and see what it reveals about your attitudes.

Your personal view of people
—and what to do about it

If your profile tends toward the left-hand side of the chart, you tend to have strong negative feelings or reservations about *people*. If you fall in this category, be sure to follow Guidelines, the four steps prescribed below, that help you get a line on the human race. The steps are a must for you! For reasons that probably grow out of your early experiences, you take a dim view of *people*. Permitted to stand, this attitude is likely to get in your way of the mastery of people. It's difficult to work effectively with people if you hate their guts.

If your profile tends toward the right-hand side of the chart, your tendency is healthy and helpful. You may need none of the Guidelines directions. Glance over them, however. Probably because of the kind of person you are, you'll want to follow up the suggestions simply because you'll enjoy doing so.

The third possibility: your profile may tend to run between the two extremes. In this case, it is highly desirable for you to follow the recommendations. Somewhere in your experience you've picked up doubts, fears, dislikes of people of a minor character, but probably strong enough to prevent a satisfactory mastery of people.

Guidelines: four steps to winning
the human race

Four steps, four linked ideas help you complete the transformation from the paralysis of awe and dread of mankind to an attitude that will mean an exhilarating ability to relate to individuals the control of whom is the key to success in your home and business life.

As you go through the points below, remember that they are key ideas for you to absorb. They will form a solid foundation on which to build effective use of the other tools you'll read about in subsequent chapters:

1. *Get the Big Picture.* Accept as a matter of course the fact that

you belong to a wonderful race of beings. In the sixth decade of the 20th century, we humans number some 2,700,000,000 souls spread out over seven continents, from the hot tropics to the frigid northland. Our accomplishments are impressive. We have built vehicles that have breached the skies, and pierced the ocean depths. One by one, we have ripped away the veils obscuring the mysteries of the atom and the cell. We're even closing in on the secrets of life and death.

BUT—despite tremendous technological advances, despite inventions and explorations that would have seemed miraculous to our grandparents, indeed, that even seem miraculous to us, *people are still people.* Go back in time—*or forward*—ten years, a hundred or a thousand. You'll find people loving, hating, desiring and fearing the same things as today. You'll find people valuing the same things—success, status, comfort, friendship, love.

Biology and psychology are on your side

Day to day, our behavior is ruled by the eternal verities of biology and psychology. Accordingly, the tools and techniques you must wield to dominate people need not be aimed at a vast abstraction but at specific individuals—your neighbor Frank Jones, fellow worker Hank Edwards, a wife, son, brother, boss.

In other words, getting the Big Picture means getting the close-up details as well. See yourself and the human race in perspective. Replace any vestige of awe you feel by a clear-eyed objectivity that can say, along with Rudyard Kipling, "Of all a man's deeds, his greatest moment comes when he can look Mankind in the eye and say, 'Hail, Brother.'"

2. *Understand what it means to be human.* Every once in a while, an individual tries to pull out of the human race. That's what Henry Thoreau did when he went off to live in the splendid solitude of Walden Pond. It didn't work as a permanent solution. After two years, Thoreau was back in civilization, living the only life that can have meaning, one among fellow humans.

Over 200 years ago, Samuel Butler said it neatly: "A man by himself is in bad company."

People who think the way to win the human race is to leave it have discovered they are wrong. "I'm giving up this rat race," is the out the weak sisters give themselves. Eventually they discover they've packed their troubles along with their supplies, learn they'd do much better to take their stand in the world of men.

It's people who make our world and our life. This is a biological and psychological fact. Our lives become meaningful and worthwhile only in relation to people. "Man is a social animal," said Spinoza. The Bible tells us, "It is not good that man should live alone."

To be human means to live the life you have: to respond to what you perceive and observe, to appreciate people, and to be willing to live your life as a human being among your fellows.

Accept the fact that people are both good and bad, weak and strong, responsible and irresponsible. Learn that no matter what kind of person an individual is, he's subject to immutable laws of biology and psychology, laws that your human relations tools will help you take advantage of to the fullest.

3. *Learn to love mankind—passionately.* Dr. Harrison B. Taylor, a consultant for the management firm of Rogers, Slade & Hill, recently told a meeting of 300 wives of business executives: "One of the keys to a happy successful home is a real genuine interest in people."

"Interest in people" is important. Yet, it is only the first rung of the ladder you can mount in the development of your feeling towards your fellow human beings. Here are the other rungs of the ladder that can take you to the heights of regard for mankind:

When you mount this ladder, you're in for some exciting vistas . . .

> love of people
> strong affection for people
> liking for people
> interest in people

What happens when you love the human race

"Man is nothing else than a sack of dung, the food of worms," said St. Bernard, the 12th-century cleric.

Jonathan Swift, in *Gulliver's Travels*, describes man as, "The most pernicious race of little odious vermin that nature ever suffered to crawl upon the surface of the earth." Dim views of the human race, it must be said in all honesty, are not infrequent. Many men, out of bitterness, disillusion or despair, have castigated their own species.

Another group of essayists, novelists, philosophers, poets expressed a mixed appraisal of their fellows. "What is man? Half beast, half angel." Thus wrote the German poet Joachim Evers 200 years ago.

Finally, we have those who have expressed their love and admiration for mankind. Robert Frost, undoubtedly one of our greatest modern poets, wrote his own epitaph, and in so doing, summed up his benign outlook on humanity: "I had a lover's quarrel with the world."

Sophocles, on his play *Antigone*, says, "There are many wonderful things in nature, but the most wonderful of all is man."

The idea that there is something special about man has always been with us. The Bible contributes to this idea. The Book of Genesis tells us, "God created man in his own image, in the image of God created he him."

When you love people, you feel close to them. When you feel close, you understand them, become aware of their needs, their feelings. You know what makes them tick. Their sore points become obvious to you, the things that they're proud about, and that which motivates them also becomes obvious.

Abraham Lincoln was said to be "a man of the people." It was this sense of being "of the people" that made him one of our greatest Presidents, and one of our greatest human beings.

Do you have to be of Presidential stature to develop a kinship with your fellow-man? Not at all. Note the case of Geraldine Englehard.

Gerry Engelhard is a long-time employee of one of New York's largest publishing firms, chief operator of their phone service. She's the kind of warm, outgoing person that people are drawn to instinctively. People come to her seeking her advice about their personal problems. A fellow employee once kidded her: "Gerry, you act as though everybody is your relative." Said Gerry, "That's just the way I feel."

It's not a new idea. As a matter of fact, it's about 2000 years old; we're all brothers under the skin. Understand and accept this one idea, and you'll never have to worry about your fellow humans again.

4. *Dedicate yourself to winning the human race.* To be human means, above all, to accept the challenge of your humanity, to take advantage of your own ambitions for achievement.

Dr. Karl S. Bernhardt, in *Practical Psychology*, says

Whether it is due to inborn nature, or, as is more likely, trained into us by social custom and education, there is a universal tendency to
strive to excel and succeed, to win out ahead of others, or to overcome
obstruction or difficulty.

Use this tendency in your own behalf.

Don't hesitate to set goals and to strive to achieve them. Be prepared for setbacks but resolve to continue your efforts, confident of
eventual success.

As human beings, few of us are ever content merely to survive.
Each of us is blessed by the urge to aspire and achieve. See your life as
an opportunity, a chance to realize a great adventure and a great victory.

"Make no small plans," said the genius of steel, Andrew Carnegie.
To achieve mastery of people you want to play to win—and plan to
win—big.

▶ Recap ◀

The highlights of this chapter:

The tool we've been talking about: Your attitude toward people—
an important key to drawing you closer to your fellow human beings.
Once you replace negative feelings for people by positive ones, you can
understand them better, and eliminate the psychological obstacles that
often come between a would-be leader and those he would like to
master.

How and when to use it: This is an easy one. You don't have to
look for opportunities to use this tool. You have it with you, always. It
always works for you.

How to develop it: There are four *guidelines:*

1. Get the Big Picture—see mankind in reasonable perspective.

2. Understand what it means to be human—be eager to live your
life as a human being among your fellows.

3. Learn to love mankind—passionately—the groundwork for your
effort was laid down by The Master some two thousand years ago.

4. Dedicate yourself to winning the human race—accept the challenge of your humanity, which, in its most universal form, means to
want to excel.

chapter 3

Howard Fabrey (not his real name for reasons that will soon become obvious) was a teller in a downtown Cleveland bank. As an employee you would have rated him poor. Notations by his boss on his performance rating form read like this:

"Knows the work but doesn't get along with the other tellers. Is generally uncooperative. Has an unpleasant manner that has caused customers to make complaints about him."

You don't have to know much about banking to realize that Howard Fabrey's future at the bank could have been written on the point of a pin.

But an unexpected development changed the course of Howard's career, and life. Howard had a mild nervous breakdown. Difficulty in sleeping, stomach upsets and constant feelings of tension suddenly culminated in his fainting at his teller's cage one summer afternoon.

A week later, Howard was

achieve new heights of self-awareness — and improve your approach to people

back on the job, apparently none the worse for his experience. Then, over a period of months, fellow workers noticed a strange transformation taking place. Howard was seen to smile while talking to the boss. He engaged in amiable chit chat, his manner was pleasant, more relaxed. Twice within a week, customers made a point of complimenting bank officers on the courtesy and helpfulness of one of their employees—meaning none other than Howard Fabrey himself!

The head of the Personnel Department nodded and smiled at the glowing report Howard's boss made of his improved job performance. The Personnel head did not feel it proper to reveal the real explanation for the teller's amazing metamorphosis.

The simple fact was, Howard's near breakdown had been a godsend in disguise. His doctor had sent him to a psychotherapist. Under the healing influence of modern counseling techniques, Howard's case could be chalked up as one more triumph for psychological healing.

Howard's cure—and everybody's

To a good friend who finally brought himself to ask Howard for an explanation the teller said, "I understand myself better. With my therapist's help I realized for the first time that I was doing things that got people's backs up. I realized I had attitudes and values that were wrong. By becoming more and more aware of the kind of person I really was, I've been able to become more and more the kind of person I want to be."

Case histories of individuals receiving professional psychotherapy show even more startling improvements than Howard Fabrey's. But no matter how modest or how extreme the improvement in the individual, *the means are always the same.* Howard Fabrey's own explanation hit it right on the button: "By becoming more and more aware of the kind of person I really was—" Self-understanding! It's the key to managing our affairs with those about us!

Few of us are likely to suffer from the handicaps of self-ignorance to the same degree that Howard Fabrey did. But it's the rare individual whose ignorance of himself doesn't get in his way. His peace of mind, and his relationships with others—the very individuals on whom his career and personal well-being depend—both suffer.

What you'll get from this chapter

I'm not going to kid you. I don't want you for one moment to believe that the few minutes you'll spend reading this chapter can substitute for the hours of professional guidance administered in therapeutic counseling such as Howard Fabrey got. Nevertheless, this chapter can be the most eye-opening, the most rewarding bit of reading you ever set your eyes on. The ideas and the devices you will find here have been carefully chosen to help you to win new heights of self-awareness. When you achieve these objectives, when you gain new insights into yourself, major improvements in your approach to people —and how you handle them—must inevitably result!

Let me spell out exactly how this will happen:

1. *You will recognize your own tendencies.* Every one of us has special and personal ways of responding to people. One person responds to those in authority unquestioningly, even meekly. Another will simmer with a strong resentment that may break out into the open at the slightest provocation. After reading this chapter, you will have a much clearer idea of your human relations attitudes—for example, your attitude towards people above you, and those who are subordinate to you, on the job, in social and community situations, and so on.

2. *You will be able to empathize with others.* The old adage, "Step into the other fellow's shoes to see how he feels," is good advice. The only trouble is, it's practically impossible to do unless you really understand his feelings. As you become more aware of your own inner feelings, you become ten times more capable of seeing things from another person's viewpoint. "I never could understand another man's courage," said Lawrence of Arabia, "until I committed my first brave act." What England's great patriot discovered about courage is true of other human feelings.

3. *You will understand how your attitudes help create attitudes in others.* I overheard this conversation coming from the other side of a supermarket foodbin recently: "Mrs. Henry sure wears the pants in that family." I happen to know Mr. and Mrs. Henry. It's quite true, Mrs. Henry is the more active and enterprising of the two. Why? Because Mr. Henry is a mild, unaggressive individual, suffering from what a psychologist might call *overdependency.* His failure to take the initiative *forces Mrs. Henry to do so.*

Here's another example: "People are so unfriendly!" a young college graduate told me, in describing his first weeks in a new job. What the young man didn't realize was that his own aloof superior manner frightened people off, and made them seem unfriendly.

At any rate you're going to love this chapter. It's about your favorite subject—*YOU*. And it's about you because *you yourself* are among the most potent of all human relations tools. As you gain in self-knowledge, and use your self-knowledge wisely, expertly, nothing can withstand you—*and no one will want to*.

However, the exciting fact about self-knowledge is this: although thousands of people have been promoting it for untold centuries, only in our own time has it become a practical objective! The discoveries of Sigmund Freud, and the psychologists who followed the trail he blazed, put self-knowledge within reach of all of us.

Shortly, you will be provided with a trio of self-analysis instruments that you can use to get through to the inner you. You will be able, for the first time, to understand things about yourself that are true *only* for you. And you will then be able to appreciate yourself for the individual you are. The three "mind probes" begin on page 31.

But, first, let us examine the nature of the inner world of which Freud was the modern Columbus.

The three inhabitants of your inner world

To understand yourself, you must give up the idea that this inner world of yours has but one citizen. The "I," is not a simple, single entity. One of Dr. Freud's great contributions to understanding of self is his concept of the makeup of the "I." Freud believed that the mind of the human being is made up of not one, but three elements, all co-existing and interacting with one another:

. . . the *id*, the instinctual force of life, the original libidinal or love force;

. . . the *ego*, the executive force that deals with the external world of reality;

. . . the *super-ego*, the conscience, the disciplinary force, that is superior to, and capable of coercing, the ego.

A major value of Freud's scheme is that it explains how a person can be wracked by inner conflict. For example, Dr. Leopold Stein, a well-known English psychiatrist and author, tells of a patient he calls Judith, suffering from anxiety brought on by violent quarrels with her husband. Even when her husband Robert began to go blind, she couldn't stop quarreling with him. Yet, she claimed to love him devoutly. Actually, it was the three-way pull of the forces governing her mental life—the id, ego and super-ego, that brought her almost to the brink of insanity.

At this point you may say, "Stop. Hold everything. What does all this Freudian mish-mash have to do with the business of self-understanding, and working with and mastering people?"

The answer is, *it's crucial.* Unless you understand that you are *not* a simple, uncomplicated being—*nor is anyone else*—your self-knowledge, and your understanding of others will always be an oversimplification. The point here isn't to make a Freudian psychologist out of you, but merely to provide a brief background you can use to bring understanding to the daily situations in which you find yourself. Before you can deal with people, you have to understand them—and yourself as well.

Fortunately, modern psychology provides us with another concept, that, taken with Freud's idea of the id, ego and super-ego, takes us still further down the vital road of self-understanding. In recent years, psychologists have become aware of a particularly important bit of portrait painting every one of us does. We don't use paints or brushes for this masterpiece, yet it is almost constantly before our mind's eye. It's called the self-image. For most of us, this picture is one of the dominant influences of our lives. Here's what it can do. . . .

The self-image casts its spell

"Will you please let out these pants?" Fred Frawley asks his wife.

"But those are the slacks you bought this morning," objects Mrs. Frawley. "Fred, when are you going to stop buying pants with a 36-inch waist? You've been a 40 for years!"

What makes Fred Frawley persist in his illogical behavior? The answer is, he *sees himself* as a youthful 36. For each of us, the self-image provides a view of ourselves that includes everything from a waist measurement to our mental capacities.

When we don't see ourselves clearly, lucidly, we're in trouble—

more trouble than we can get out of simply by letting out the waistband of our trousers a few inches.

The self-image is a vital concept. It explains a great deal about our behavior and our outlook on the world. See how a person's self-image can help—or hinder—his dealings with people:

Portrait #1—Hank Blake. "An outstanding employee," is the way Hank was described by his boss. He could operate almost any machine in the shop with an expert hand, was dependable and interested in his work. "Sure to go places," his fellow employees agreed. Finally, the break that everyone expected for Hank came his way. His boss called him in one morning and said, "Hank, my assistant is moving over into the Molding Division. I need an assistant foreman. A ten percent increase in pay goes with the spot. How about it?"

Hank was silent for a moment, then, "Sorry, Boss. I don't want the job." Why had Hank turned down the promotion? He had an easy explanation for his friends: "Just didn't want the headaches," he said.

The truth of the matter was, *Hank's self-image got in his way.* He saw himself only as a worker, accordingly couldn't take the step out of rank-and-file into higher echelons.

Portrait #2—Bill Fernald. Bill started in with a West Coast camera company about five years ago. "I didn't start at the bottom," says Bill jokingly, "I started below that." Actually, his first job was in the shipping department, as general cleanup boy. Pretty soon the other men in shipping got on to Bill's hopes—and laughed themselves silly. "The kid thinks he's going to be a bigshot around here," they told each other with derision.

But the kid was right. Inside of five brief years, Bill Fernald at the age of 24 became the youngest division manager in the company. Just last year, at the age of 28, he was given the job of executive vice president. As he sat in the armchair in his plush office, to have his picture taken for a trade paper article, he said, "You know, the day I walked into this plant, I saw myself sitting in this chair." His self-image helped get him where he wanted to go. He *saw* himself as a top executive. That proved to be half the battle.

As we've said, the way you see yourself is an important factor in your relations with others. Let's look into more of the fascinating facets of the person called "you."

Exploring inner space

This chapter is not a do-it-yourself psychiatry kit. There is no such thing. These pages will not help you to psychoanalyze yourself, or tell you how to cure your own neuroses if you have any. But it can show you some important truths about yourself. And it will give you guidance on what to do about them, and how to use them so as to improve your ability to command people.

The book of *Genesis* recounts how Adam hid in the Garden of Eden after eating the forbidden fruit. And God called out, "Adam, where are thou?"

Scholars have pondered why God, knowing all things, should ask Adam to reveal his hiding place. And the answer they have given is that *God* knew where Adam was; he wanted to be sure that *Adam* knew.

The need for self-knowledge is as old as history. How many of us really know who we are?

The experiments of psychologists repeatedly remind us how little we know about ourselves. Amazingly, we can be, and often are, unaware of our own feelings, emotions, beliefs, goals. It's as though, in the world of the mind, there are no mirrors.

Tests performed by Professor Werner Wolff of Bard College dramatize our unfamiliarity with ourselves. He asked people to identify faceless pictures of themselves and their friends. The average person had trouble picking himself out of a crowd. People had better luck labeling the pictures of acquaintances!

If you have ever seen movies of yourself or listened to a recording of your voice, you have probably said to yourself, "Is *that* me?"

We are astonished by this unfamiliarity with our own outer shell— our appearance and voice. But it is even more significant that we know so little about our inner selves.

How we lie to ourselves

So great is the human need for love and approval that we even deceive ourselves, when necessary, into believing that we deserve them. In many cases we don't even know that we are protecting ourselves. As we mentioned earlier, Freud pointed out that many of our actions are motivated by the unconscious mind which stands like a guardian angel to protect our image of ourselves. See how our protection of our self-image forces us to behave in ways that are bound to damage our relations with people.

. . . we make excuses, alibiing ourselves out of situations. "I did it because. . . ." And we think we have provided good and substantial reasons for our behavior. But others see through this maneuver easily.

. . . we disown the fault and say it's the other fellow's doing. And as you know, no one likes a poor sport.

. . . we take it out on a subordinate to avoid looking at ourselves. The "unreasonable, tyrannical boss" is one of the most unloved people in the world.

These defenses help us deceive ourselves and retain our image of ourselves as important and productive people. Unfortunately, these defenses also bar the way to accurate and creative self-understanding, and to establishing productive relationships with others.

These protective safety devices, operating from our unconscious mind, work automatically. We have to be very skillful if we want to sneak up on ourselves and take a quick look.

Our hidden motivations

Take the case of a San Francisco elevator operator. He's five foot seven inches, weighs 250 pounds. He makes all kinds of resolutions about drinking and diets. On the surface, he has every reason for sticking to his resolves. Yet, he is powerless to carry them out. Some internal pressure apparently forces him away from what he consciously wants to do.

Most of us, at some time or other, have had the same sort of trouble with a particular chore. We promise ourselves we'll get to it soon, but the opportunity never seems to arise. The storm windows don't go up early, or the car doesn't get anti-freeze until it's almost too late. We avoid having a showdown with a colleague who has been giving us a rough time. We fail to take the steps that will put us in a position to show the Boss what we can do.

Once you know how your defenses operate, you need not be an enemy to yourself. But first you must overcome the barriers to self-understanding. Only then can you make the unconscious an ally and not an enemy—utilizing its power to help you live up to your fullest potential in the challenging job of mastering people.

The techniques for studying personality are very complicated. To penetrate to real depth, you may have to call in the expert. But some of the instruments used by the psychologist to probe into character can be adapted for your own use. Here are three outstanding ones, the trio of "mind probes" I promised you earlier.

Using the instruments of self-analysis

Do not expect any magic key to give you the whole answer.

As the noted psychiatrist, Dr. Lawrence Kubie, has pointed out: "Moments of discovery . . . usually come in small increments." The following methods of self-study are useful because each, in its own way, helps to provide an outline sketch of your self-image. Future observations will help you fill in the picture with additional strokes that reflect your responses to living. But right from the start you will acquire a new way of looking at yourself.

Three roads to self-knowledge

We do not suggest that you attempt to use all the three instruments below at once. Read the section as a unit, then select one of the methods. Ask yourself which seems to you to be most interesting, most suitable to your needs, and most likely to yield new information. Your choice may be influenced by the amount of time you have available right now, since some of the instruments require more time than others. In any case, pick one and get to work on it immediately.

You will never meet a more intriguing personality than your own. Get to know yourself now!

I. The autobiographical approach

Some people may find it fruitful to probe their past, to uncover the critical incidents that helped determine what they are today. This can be done fairly easily, starting out with your earliest memories about the important people in your life. Here are some key questions:

What was your father like?

How did you react to him as a person?

Did you resent his discipline then and did you later come to understand his motives?

What hopes did he have for you?

What dreams did you dream together about the future?

Do you find yourself acting in some ways toward your children as he did toward you?

And what about your mother, what kind of person was she?

How did you get along with her?

Were you her favorite child?

And how about your teachers and other school authorities, what were your reactions to them?

Be honest in your answers. All children have conflicts with their parents and other adults. Mature people can recognize the nature of the conflicts and understand now what they might not have understood then. If you have this understanding, you are less likely to continue to act out your childhood conflicts in adult life. Merely raising these questions with yourself now, in your mature years, can give you new and insightful answers. For example:

Ernie Haymes was a Chicago taxi driver. He got started on a line of self-questioning similar to the one above. Giving the queries considerable thought, he finally realized, "As a kid, I just couldn't stand being told what to do. I guess I hated anyone who represented authority. That went for everyone from my old man to the cop on the beat."

In the course of his thinking about his feelings about authority, he had a further amazing insight: "I guess it's because of the way I felt about authority that I eased into the job of driving a hack. Behind the wheel, you're pretty much your own boss."

Ernie came to realize that his feelings were rooted in a past that he had more or less outgrown. His dislike of authority had largely mellowed. . . .

With this new insight, he was able to make an entirely new career for himself. He had always been a good car mechanic. He went to technical school for a while, brushed up on some basic courses, got a job in a large Ford service station. Today, Ernie is a partner in the business. He is able not only to have good relations with people in authority, but also—and this is extremely important to the relationship between self-understanding and the mastery of people—he is *a hundred times more capable of wielding authority over others!*

This is the way self-understanding can open doors, create new opportunities, give you a power over your own career, and over other people, that might otherwise never have materialized.

Reactions to all kinds of authority are often a continuation of the relationship you had with your parents. A study of your own past can help you better handle the present and—most important—it can aid in building a better foundation for the future.

Don't look just for dramatic and easily recalled memories from your past. These may be important, but they're apt to give you a distorted picture. Take a look at the small details that stay with you, that recur whenever you think about the past. These undoubtedly played a part in shaping your self-image, and are the keys to better self-understanding, and better understanding of others.

II. Note the recent extremes

Our highs and lows—the extremes of our emotions and feelings—often provide a current clue to the core that lies hidden in our everyday controlled behavior. The unusual is, in effect, an exaggeration of the usual.

We make a mistake if we dismiss the off-beat, unusual events in our lives. "That's not like me," we say and discount an incident completely. But an analysis of the times we get angrier than we ever supposed was possible or experienced joy beyond our fondest expectation reveals what we are. This *is* like you—when you are at your you-est!

Try this experiment for a week. Keep a diary of your unusual reactions. It might be just a fleeting moment of feeling: exhilaration, anger, frustration. Or it might be a lift of spirits or a depression that lasts all day. It doesn't matter how long it lasts. What counts is that, *a.* it is stronger than usual; *b.* that *you* experienced it.

Here are the steps that will help you examine and uncover its significance:

1. *Record it.* Jot down the feeling and as many of the details of its cause as you can possibly capture. Don't be concerned about language, so long as you can be certain that you have enough to bring it all back to mind later.

2. *Accumulate a variety.* Before you examine and review your record, list at least five different types of situations. If a week does not provide enough items, take a longer period.

3. *Analyze the contents.* At the end of a week or two you should

have recorded enough separate items to form some picture. These guides will help you analyze them:

 . . . is there any common thread or pattern?

 . . . is there a special time of the day, a particular type of individual or problem that recurs?

 . . . what is your role in each situation?

 . . . are you the bystander or an active participant?

 . . . what did you contribute to the good items? (For example, did you help save a person in distress, speak up in a situation that took moral courage, and so on?)

 . . . what did you contribute to the bad ones?

 . . . do you think you can predict your behavior better now than you could before?

The point of these questions is to increase your self-awareness in specific, concrete ways. Review those events that involved other people, replaying them in your mind like a movie. But with one big difference: *change your role.* Try to picture yourself as the *other* person. See if the story unfolds in the same way. Would you have made him as angry—or happy—as he made you in the original scene? You'll learn much about yourself by stepping into the shoes of the people to whom you react strongly.

Done properly, reviewing your "Emotional Diary" can be a fascinating and rewarding process. This is self-analysis of a particularly worthwhile kind, because it avoids the approach of the parlor psychologist who tells you all about your "subconscious mind" by aping the techniques and jargon of the professional. The "Emotional Diary" gives you the opportunity to make a straightforward analysis of your emotional reactions on a common sense level.

A major benefit of this exercise is to heighten your sensitivity to your relationships with people. It tells you what your actions and responses are, how others will react to you. Then, by switching roles, you can gain insight into the other persons' feelings, and how you may have looked to them!

What better preparation can there be for understanding and coping with the emotion-charged situations we find ourselves up against—a depressed colleague who needs encouragement, an overenthusiastic youngster who needs to be brought down to earth gently, an obstinate boss whose views require enlightenment.

III. Change of routine

We all tend to become blind to the familiar and accustomed things around us. Until a visit from a stranger jolts us into looking at our surroundings through his eyes, we may remain unaware of the most obvious facts.

More important, we often lose ourselves in the rush of daily pressures, becoming insensitive to our own reactions. Anne Morrow Lindbergh felt this need to get away from daily pressures—the running of a home, the endless committee meetings, the demands of her five children.

To rediscover herself, she decided to break the pattern of routine. She took a few weeks at the beach in new surroundings. Her beautiful, sensitive book, *Gift from the Sea*, describes some of the discoveries she made about herself:

"When one is a stranger to oneself, then one is estranged from others too. If one is out of touch with oneself, then one cannot touch others. . . . For me, the core, the inner spring, can best be refound through solitude."

Maybe you can't take a few weeks at the shore but you can accomplish the same thing in other ways:

. . . go through an entire day as if you were about to leave the job or the community. How would you act, what would you notice if you felt that you would never be here again?

. . . pretend that you had to explain all of your actions and decisions to a child. Go through a day imagining the questions a 12-year-old might ask about your way of responding to the common situations that come up.

. . . spend a day alone, with no fixed program. If possible, and if the family will understand, take a solo trip in your car, letting your mood determine your destination.

. . . examine new by-ways. Take a new route even if it's only on the way to work.

. . . take a trip back to your old hometown and search out remembered landmarks.

. . . spend a day pretending that you and one of your subordinates have switched roles. Try to act as he would.

By changing your point of view for a day, you can often open your eyes and see yourself and your behavior in a new light. The more frequently you get out of your rut and look around you, the more freshness and insight you gain.

Three steps to a handsomer self-portrait

Now you want to put the things you've discovered about yourself to work. Whether you've used one or all of the three self-probes we've described, the findings, to be of value, must be incorporated into your self-image.

Just follow the simple steps described below, and you'll not only improve your self-image, but you'll gain increased inner ease, and greater self-confidence in relation to others. Both these benefits play a major role in helping you manage people. Here's what to do:

1. *Convert the negative elements.* Perhaps you've uncovered some *negative* things about yourself. For example, you may discover that you resent authority, or that you tend to be selfish in your dealings with people, or that you find it difficult to assert a point of view vigorously.

On discovering unfavorable elements about themselves, some people say, "That's the way I am and I guess I'm stuck." It may *seem* so. Fortunately, you needn't accept any such finding. The first thing to remember is this:

The negative elements in the make-up of most people are based on events that happened a long time ago. Take one instance we mentioned above, inability to assert a point of view vigorously.

Frank Koral was an assistant foreman in a woodworking company near Washington, D. C., doing just a so-so job. His inability stemmed from an unfortunate childhood situation. His father had been a domineering tyrant who had walked over every member of the family, not excluding young Frank.

Remind yourself that the negative elements don't fit the present you. Frank developed the insight about his undesirable trait, and was willing to take the remedy recommended for it. He said to himself, "My inability to assert myself is a result of what happened in my family life 15 years ago. It's an undesirable obstacle, and interferes with my leadership of the men in my department, and with my chances of becoming foreman. Since I know this feeling doesn't reflect my present situation, I intend to get rid of it. I'm as capable of asserting myself as anyone else is." '

Repeat the dose as needed. Don't expect to rid yourself of an undesirable element in one self-confrontation like Frank's. He went through the process repeatedly. But after only a few weeks he began to detect a favorable change in his ability to hold up his end of an argument. And his ability on this score continued to increase with time.

Since you now have an insight into yourself, since you understand the illogical, neurotic basis for the undesirable feeling, keep reminding yourself how inappropriate it is *for the person you are right now.* To pin down your elimination of these undesirable elements, make it your business to incorporate *the opposite of the undesirable trait* into your self-portrait.

Many people do this unconsciously. Watch the next Salvation Army charity worker with his coin box you see in the street. Watch a blind man with his cup. A hurrying housewife, a business executive, a secretary on her lunch hour will stop to drop a coin.

Do you think these are generous, warm-hearted people? Unlikely. More possible is the fact that they are the opposite. *But*—the nickel or dime they're handing out is the purchase price for the feeling that they are charitable and generous!

You can follow their good example—and it needn't be limited to depositing coins in collection boxes. Look for ways and means in your everyday life to make the moves that will help you prove to yourself that the negative elements that have lingered on from childhood simply no longer apply to you now in your greater maturity and with your greater insight.

2. *Extend and expand the positive elements your self-analysis has revealed.* Ann Bayard is an executive secretary in the New York home office of a large chemical company. She used the "Diary of Emotions" device and discovered that the things about her job that gave her the greatest pleasure were those in which she showed initiative and creativity.

She had never thought of herself as a particularly creative person. "After all," she said, "secretarial work doesn't give a girl much of an opportunity for originality."

Nevertheless, the insight she had gained through her Emotional Diary made her realize that she was more original and creative than she had thought. Accordingly, she cast about for some means of exercising this quality.

Note carefully the progression of events here: Ann had discovered a hidden ability in herself. Next, she incorporated it into her self-image, *began to see herself* as a creative person.

In her search for ways to take advantage of her new-found trait, she decided that she had always been interested in photography and would pursue it as a hobby. She took a course given at the "Y" in her neighborhood. She proved to be a particularly apt pupil. She now finds she can earn as much as an additional $100 and more a month selling her pictures to newspapers, magazines, and other commercial publications.

But the benefits of her improved self-image didn't stop even there. The head of the personnel department in her company heard of her success with photography and asked her whether she'd like to start a hobby club for the company. Ann agreed to do so. Now she's a junior executive with great prospects for the future, head of her company's recreation program, and full of plans for building the morale and job satisfaction of employees.

The important thing—aside from the money and increased prestige —is the tremendous amount of satisfaction she derives from exercising her heretofore hidden ability. She's arrived in great style.

In the same way, you can develop and apply the favorable things you have learned about yourself. Incorporate them into your self-image, remind yourself frequently of your originality, your capability as a conversationalist, your particular ability to organize, and so on, as the case may be.

And then take the final step: look about you in your work, in your community for ways and means to apply this talent productively so as to give you both profit and pleasure.

3. *Remember: a frame helps make a picture.* Every artist understands this principle. Put it to work for your self-image. If you see yourself as a person with a talent for being able to put people at ease and relax them, *put yourself in situations where this talent will have meaning.* Join organizations, become active in groups in which this trait will be of value. Fraternal clubs, civic and religious organizations, little theatre companies—the organizations and the opportunities for you to demonstrate to people what you have on the ball are endless.

▶ RECAP ◀

The highlights of this chapter:

The tool we've been talking about: self-knowledge, your understanding of yourself. Self-understanding is of critical importance in the mastery of people because self-ignorance is a major cause of "foot-in-mouth disease," of major errors in dealing with people. And self-understanding is a time-honored bridge to the understanding of others.

How and when to use it: You apply it in situations where (a) you're not sure of your own feelings and (b) you're not sure of the other person's feelings. Self-understanding is the key to the *emotional* aspect of human relations, usually the critical factor in difficult relationships.

How to develop it: Three specific instruments have been provided for the heightening of your self-awareness:

1. *The autobiographical analysis.* By reviewing and reappraising your past, you can gain new insights into the present and future.

2. *The Emotional Diary.* By keeping a diary of your emotions and analyzing the contents, you can achieve new revelations into the innermost thoughts of yourself and other people. It can help explain past difficulties you may have had in dealing with people and solve problem areas that may have dogged you heretofore.

3. *Changing your routine.* This mental exercise can open your eyes so that you can see yourself and your behavior in fresh light. This new view of yourself can help you establish new and productive relationships, and mend frayed relationships of long standing.

The final, and payoff step: you incorporate the favorable, desirable, elements you've uncovered about yourself into your self-image, then put this self-portrait to work for you! Let it give you increased self-confidence, and greatly magnified success in your social and on-the-job contacts and relationships with people.

And now we go on to the next tool, one thought to be the most difficult of all to wield, but one you can convert to a powerful asset. The tool: *The ability to size up people.*

chapter 4

There are times when you'd give your right arm to get the lowdown on an individual:

"That was a pretty good job," Tom's boss says. The boss sounds approving. But Tom wonders, does the boss *really* think his performance has been successful? Or is his statement merely a bland kiss-off, hiding disappointment?

At home you try to enlist your neighbor in a project to buy an empty lot that adjoins both your properties. Your idea is that you purchase the lot jointly, then divide it on a 50–50 basis. Your neighbor says, "Let me think about it a few days." You suspect he isn't the least bit interested. On the other hand, you think he might try to pull a fast one, and buy the whole parcel on his own, while you're waiting for his decision. If only you could tell . . .

Or take this instance. A stranger walks in on you and suggests a tempting business proposal. He's personable, well spoken. Yet you're not sure

how to

become more

perceptive

about people

— and capitalize

on what

you learn

you've got him sized up properly. If only you could be certain you had him figured right . . .

To know is to control

It's almost impossible to exaggerate the importance of being able to judge people accurately, to know what an individual is thinking or feeling in a given situation. Everyone agrees it's an ability that is crucial in human relations. Yet, the chorus is almost as unanimous in saying, "Sensitivity to people is an inborn talent. You either have it, or you don't."

This chapter contradicts that popular belief. Go through these pages, take the ideas to heart, follow the recommendations, and your ability to sense what people are thinking and feeling will jump sky high.

In Chapter 6, you'll learn about the opportunities you gain when you learn to tune in on the *group* mind—the people down at the office, your club or church group. This chapter develops the methods you can use to perceive clearly what goes on inside an individual's mind—even when he's doing his best to play it deadpan, or to hide his intentions.

When you size up a person accurately, you're in a position to get positive benefits:

You can pick the right man for a job—either a temporary but critical assignment, or a permanent place on your staff.

You won't make the mistake of placing your bets on an untrustworthy person.

You can sidestep the sharper, the man who's out to trick you, financially or otherwise.

Finally, you gain much broader effectiveness in dealing with people in general.

Read—and reap.

The clues exist—
if you know where to look

The first principle to learn in developing your perceptivity: living creatures of all kinds, up and down the evolutionary scale reveal themselves by subtle clues or signs. Witness:

Nineteen-year old Jean Lester, daughter of a South African farmer, was showing off her ability to handle her pet leopard. As friends watched, she opened the barred gate and called the feline to her.

The huge cat crept from its cage. But suddenly the play turned into near tragedy. According to *Life* magazine's report of the incident: "The beast's eyes suddenly widened, a sure sign of danger." And then the pet leopard turned into a killer, charging murderously at his terrified keeper. If not for the fast action of her father, who beat the animal off, Jean Lester would have suffered more than the lacerations of the shoulder that resulted.

Note the phrase, "The beast's eyes suddenly widened, a sure sign of danger." The leopard had telegraphed its sudden surge of murderous rage. Animals often provide specific clues as to moods or impending acts. A cat's purr tells you of its contentment. The gorilla about to go into combat will beat his chest. The lion intending to charge signals the event with his outstretched tail. A well-known reptile announces his plan to strike by a characteristic whirring of his rattles.

Unveiling the human enigma

"But," you may say, "these examples are all from the animal kingdom. Human beings are more complicated, and a lot less obvious."

Not so. The fact is, human beings frequently provide clues equally as revealing, *once you learn to recognize them.*

Just ask a poker player.

I did, in a recent conversation with one of the country's outstanding card experts. He told me, "Almost every player gives himself away —if you study him carefully.

"For example, I was in a game yesterday with a fellow whose raises had driven everyone else out. We were playing 7-card stud, and he had four hearts showing. Chances were fairly good that he had a fifth heart buried that would give him a winning flush. That was the way everyone else had him figured. But I stuck to the end, and beat him out with a pair of aces.

"The poor fellow never knew why I called his bluff. The fact is, I was *sure* he didn't have the flush. How did I know? Simple. Whenever he bluffed, he tapped on the table with a ring he wore on his right hand."

Poker players, the good ones, that is, are usually expert at reading the clues that people give of what they're thinking and feeling. When you improve your ability to "read" people, you can tell a lot more about them than simply whether they're four-flushing or not.

The triple trap—
how to avoid misjudgment

One way to learn about understanding people is to study the *wrong* way—the style of those who indulge in what I call the "wiseguy" approach. This attempt, foredoomed to failure, is marked by its rigidity. Its practitioners boast of "100% surefire accuracy." Here are three methods that have one thing in common. They're undependable, as likely to get you *into* trouble as to get you out:

"I can always tell when a man is lying by watching his mouth. Just watch the way he tightens up around the lips. It's a dead giveaway."

The fault here is *generalization*. Avoid it like the plague.

No doubt *some* people, when lying, betray their tensions by a tightening of the muscles around the mouth. But to proceed from *some*—a completely vague and unspecific number that might range from 5% to 50 or 60%—to the statement that *every* man gives himself away in this fashion is just downright naïve. It's like the faithful wife in Bocaccio's *Decameron,* who thought all men had birthmarks on their stomachs because her husband did.

The second pitfall to avoid: "You can always tell when John is moody. He picks at his fingernails."

The fault here is *uniformity*. Avoid applying it to individual human behavior, because people can be as changeable as the sky at sunset. Few people are so robotlike that they *always* resort to the same giveaway signals.

There will come a time in John's moodiness—it may be particularly intense, or focus on a strongly-felt situation—when instead of picking his fingernails, he will become almost apathetic or lethargic. And if you're watching for his fingernail signal, you may suddenly be caught in an emotional blowup for which you were completely unprepared.

Here's an example of the third phony approach to understanding people: "You can tell a dishonest man because when he uses hypothetical figures, he'll use even ones—two, four, six, and so on."

The annals of management contain a classic example of this same type of ineffective judgment. It's been told with various famous men as the main character, ranging from Jay Gould to Henry Ford. I find it difficult to believe of the latter, whose judgment of men was usually keen and perceptive. But here goes:

A leading industrialist invites a young and promising job applicant out to lunch. At the restaurant, the young hopeful orders mashed potatoes, and as soon as they're placed in front of him, he commences to sprinkle the plate liberally with salt.

"He just won't do," decides the business executive, "he's too impulsive, acts without taking stock first."

To read into an innocuous act a sign of a deep-seated character trait just doesn't make sense. It's unfair to conclude the salt-sprinkling reveals an impulsive, thoughtless nature. The plain fact may be that the young man has a taste for highly-seasoned food, or a particular affinity for salty potatoes.

The third fault of which we've given two examples is one I call *Grandmother's character recipes*. There's a tremendous amount of insight in folk wisdom. But when it comes to character analysis, folk wisdom, or I should say, *folksy wisdom* has about the same relationship to modern psychological insights as old-fashioned folk medicine—the type that treats a sore throat by application of a rag soaked in frog water—to modern medical science.

Avoid then, these three hazards: the *100% generalization*—the idea that *all* people show the same mood or character by the same signs. Remember, in one Polynesian culture, people weep in greeting and laugh at sad partings. Forsake also the error of *uniformity*—the idea that an individual will always signal the same mood in the same way. And finally, give no credence to the *old wives' approach* to analyzing character—whether it be by head bumps or any other phony means.

Judging people, face-to-face

First of all, let's talk about judging people in the ordinary conversational situation. If we fail to understand the people we come into contact with in a personal face-to-face situation, we can never hope to understand the world at large.

Right off, I can tell you that people rarely approach others with an openness to the cues in their behavior.

There's a simple reason. We're usually too absorbed with ourselves.

In some cases, we worry about how we look to the person we're talking to. We want to make a favorable impression. This is our insecurity showing.

As a result of this preoccupation with ourselves, we overlook red flag clues. I talked to a bewildered executive this morning, whose secretary had "suddenly" developed hysterics. What had gone wrong? The poor girl had been with the firm ten years. To celebrate, she had bought herself a small bouquet of flowers for her desk. Her boss failed to notice this mountain-size clue.

Then, two of her girlfriends from an adjoining office had taken her out to lunch. When she came back fifteen minutes late, her boss bawled her out. The girl simply blew up and walked out. To this moment, he doesn't know whether she'll be back. That man had practically had a message bellowed at him, yet he'd been completely oblivious.

The more self-conscious a person is, the more trouble he'll have understanding the other fellow. The more time and effort you spend on putting yourself over, the less successful you'll be at observing and understanding the other person.

Develop your sensitivity

Test yourself, as an exercise. Next time you're holding a conversation with someone, look directly at him, actually meet his eyes and concentrate. Don't let your thoughts wander, *really listen to what he's saying and how he's saying it.*

Don't respond immediately when it's your turn to speak. Use silence as a tool for digging into a person's psyche. Silence has an amazing effect on people, it makes them reveal themselves.

Try this suggestion yourself at the first opportunity. When you're in a conversation with someone, don't rush in to fill the conversational gaps. Let silence take over for a few moments. The other person will jump in to fill the verbal vacuum and almost invariably, he'll uncover himself, reveal thoughts, provide important clues that otherwise would never emerge.

Want to see how silence works in actual practice? Here's the transcript of a portion of an interview that took place in the office of an insurance officer seeking an executive assistant:

Applicant: I believe, Sir, that my experience is particularly well suited to the position you're trying to fill.

Executive: (silence)

Applicant: I've done a lot of things that would fit right in here. For example, my last boss said that attention to detail was one of my strong points.

Executive: (silence)

Applicant: Of course, my boss and I didn't get along too well. He just loaded me with responsibility. I was perfectly willing to shoulder a big load of work, but he made me responsible for a lot of things that he should have taken care of himself.

Executive: You have some trouble in assuming responsibility.

Applicant: Yes, I suppose that's true. I'm much more comfortable at a job where I just follow orders . . .

Got any doubts about the effectiveness of silence as a mood-probing, thought-revealing device? Try it on someone you know. Try it, for example, on your wife at the breakfast table tomorrow. How? Just put your newspaper down, and look at her. She'll start talking about things that are really on her mind. The point is, your silence removes obstacles from the conversational path. You unblock the road to some line of thought or feeling that the other person can, for the first time, get off his chest.

To sharpen your skill, give it a couple of trials with friends, members of your family. Then do it where it counts—with your boss, or some other key figure on the job.

And there's an additional benefit to the use of silence. You'll seem less tense, less overanxious to please.

What to look for

"But what do you look for?" a junior executive of a Philadelphia department store asked, when I was expounding on the subject of developing one's perceptions about people.

The question surprised me at first. Then I realized he had asked a shrewd question. Yes, there *are* things to look for that are not obvious. Usually when we talk of understanding people, we talk in terms of character traits. We may say a man is honest, dependable, imaginative, and so on. But there is another important order of qualities that can open up whole new avenues to understanding and handling individuals.

You won't hear many people talking about these attributes of an individual. They're fairly sophisticated concepts—in the sense that they're not the simple traditional qualities we're so used to, like dependability, courage, and so on. But the following list of "things to look for" in the words of the Philadelphia junior executive can add a whole new dimension to your view of the individuals you work with and have contact with, at home and on the job. They were suggested to me by an authority in the field of interviewing.

The eye-opening five that show you what's behind the mask

Ruth Burger is author of one of the more widely used textbooks in the demanding field of business interviewing. Her book, "The Executive Interview," can be found in most business libraries, and on the private bookshelves of many personnel executives.

I interviewed Mrs. Burger in her office on Fifth Avenue, in midtown Manhattan. Here's the gist of what this very perceptive business expert has to say about the keys to judging an individual:

. . . *tension level*. Let's say you're questioning a subordinate about a mistake that's been made. Note the amount of strain he shows. You don't get this by some kind of Grandma's mumbo jumbo, but by comparing his behavior in the present situation to his normal manner. His expression, his use of gestures, other physical signs give you your answer.

. . . *degree of openness*. How freely is he communicating? Is he weighing his words carefully? Do you sense a wariness in the way he answers questions? If the answer is yes, his hesitation probably means that *in the present situation*, at any rate, he feels threatened, he's afraid that a slip of the tongue may get him into trouble. Now you've got a hot lead. Why is he wary? Is he hiding something? What might explain his caution?

. . . *his role in the situation*. In some cases, this can be extremely revealing, but now *you* have to proceed with caution in making your judgment. Here's what I mean. The way an individual sees himself in a situation tells you a great deal about the way he feels about himself, and about the situation. For example:

A factory foreman is talking to a well-dressed, well-groomed young lady who has applied for a job as a machine operator. The foreman very soon perceives that the girl feels the job is beneath her. Her casual, offhand manner, excessive self-assurance show this. But "she needs the money" and will consent to take the job. With this insight in his possession, the foreman must now decide whether he wants to hire a girl with this kind of attitude.

. . . *rigidity of thinking.* A personnel assistant who screens job applicants told me, "I sometimes interrupt a person, and throw him a curve, just to see how he'll take it." What this skilled interviewer was getting at was the *calculated interruption,* that suddenly confronts the individual with an unexpected question. For example, to a technician who was trying to give the impression that he knew all there was to know about his specialty, came this poser: "What would be your reaction if the company suggested you go to school nights to take a refresher course?"

It's the person's reaction to a far out, essentially surprising question that can help you decide how set an individual is in his attitudes, his ideas about himself, and so on.

. . . *his value system.* Every individual has a value system that reflects his outlook on almost every aspect of life. In many cases, the value system is "inherited"—he's picked it up from his family, from his circle of friends, or from today's middle class culture of which most of us are a part.

Nevertheless, regardless of the source, an individual's value system is a significant reflection of his sense of what's right and wrong, what's good and bad in the world about him. Sometimes a person will reveal his sense of value directly: "I love to read poetry"; "History has always fascinated me."

Just as often a person will reveal his system of values unintentionally—if you listen to what he says. For example, listen to this rambling discourse of a purchasing agent of a Pittsburgh metal fabricating plant:

". . . and then this fellow came in, and I spotted him right off as a fly-by-night just by his appearance, a wrinkled suit. Then he surprised the hell out of me by giving me the most intelligent spiel on conveyor systems I'd ever heard from a salesman . . ."

The PA is easily impressed. Too easily. On the one hand, he gives too much weight to personal appearance. Next he falls hook, line and sinker for an "intelligent spiel" that may sound impressive, but in actuality, may have been memorized, and likely as not, was prepared by sales engineers back in the salesman's home office.

A man's sense of values is extremely revealing. When you know what a man thinks is important and what isn't, what matters and what doesn't, what's worthy and what isn't—you know pretty much what he's made of, from the inside out.

Small clue, great significance

Remember the old family doctor, the GP who brought medical wisdom and human warmth and reassurance to so many families in past decades? Dr. Heinrich Vogel, who many years ago had an office on 98th Street and Madison, in New York City, was of this near-vanished breed. Old Doc Vogel used to say he could diagnose a case just by the way the patient said "Come in," in answer to his knock.

Dr. Vogel didn't reveal his secret to his worshipful patients. Yet, it was a simple one. He could diagnose so expertly because he knew his patients in their *normal state*. They didn't have to run a high fever before old Doc got on to the fact that something was wrong.

You can use this same principle in developing your perceptivity. The principle is this: watch for a *change from normal*. It's particularly suited to help you detect what's on the mind of those you know fairly well.

1. How you judge

The clues you look for, the symptoms you try to spot to determine the five giveaways just described, lie in the man's appearance and manner. You watch his gestures, his posture, the amount of fidgeting he does.

The expression of his face is a particularly rewarding source of clues. The easiness and sincerity of his smile, the earnestness with which he discusses the things that are important to him, the nature of his visage when he disagrees or takes issue with you, all add up to dependable revelations of the inner man.

The approaches we've been talking about will help you "read" all kinds of people—those you know very well, those you know slightly, perfect strangers.

Some of the techniques will be more difficult to use with people who are closest to you, simply because they are the ones you can be least objective about. But by developing a fresh viewpoint, by making an effort to set aside your preconceptions or feelings about a friend or family member, and *really* listening, applying the probes described above, you'll find that you'll be able to gain better understanding of people to whom you've been closest.

You have a good idea about people you see often—colleagues on the ob, friends, members of your family. You have a fairly accurate ap- raisal of what constitutes normal behavior for them. It's because you have a clear picture of what's normal that you can make observations like this:

"My secretary seems preoccupied this morning."

"The boss is in a good mood."

"Tommy," a parent may say to a son, "you look troubled. What's wrong?"

The importance of behavior that's off the normal range, that repre- sents a change from what you might expect, is that there's a reason for it. Something has happened, and the person you're observing is worried or tense or depressed. These significant moods are detectable on the basis of the change from his prevailing mood.

When a friendly person, one who usually is carefree and converses with you easily, is withdrawn and distant, you know some negative element has thrust itself into his mind. How do you find out what it is? By tactful questioning.

With a good friend, a direct approach usually brings you the answer. You may simply ask, "Anything wrong?" Or, "You seem somewhat pre- occupied. Anything bothering you?"

Take it as a rule that will apply in nine out of ten cases: a change in a person's normal behavior pattern means that something has happened to cause the change. Now, for some people, the difference in behavior may be marked. Some people react more to events or emotional pres- sures than others. You'll have no trouble spotting the changes of this magnitude.

But other individuals, with relatively the same reasons, may show a much smaller degree of change in their manner. This may mean they're better at covering up their feelings, not that the intruding event is less serious or noteworthy.

A TV producer friend of mine whose perceptivity about people rates high told me, "I was in talking to one of my cameramen yesterday.

He's a pretty placid fellow, usually steady as a rock. But I noticed that as we talked, he stumbled over words, spoke a little more rapidly than usual. I asked him what was wrong, and he explained that his wife was seriously ill. I sent him home in a hurry . . ."

Two points emerge from this example. One is that, once you get in the habit of watching for changes in normal behavior, even the slightest sign can tell you volumes. The other suggests one of the uses to which you put your perceptions about people.

The TV executive was able to help one of his subordinates, because he had spotted the man's troubled state of mind. And this is one of the major payoffs you derive from being able to "read" people.

In other words, by your increased perceptiveness about people, you can broaden and deepen your relationships. You can be a more sympathetic boss, a more helpful colleague. Obviously, you multiply your leadership capacity a thousandfold by exercising this tool of "mind reading."

II. Observation is a habit—develop it

You can increase your sensitivity to people by practicing. You walk through a crowded room. How much do you see? Who is talking to whom? What expressions do the individuals reveal? Who are the "wall-flowers," the individuals you see at almost every gathering who have trouble mixing?

You can do the same exercise in observation anywhere—in a bus or train, at the supermarket or at a conference table at the office.

The method to develop is one that *withholds* judgment. Don't say, "Oh, there's jolly old Bill Leads talking to thoughtful Jane Benson." Don't take it for granted that Bill Leads is being his jolly self or you'll miss the whole array of clues he's creating. Don't assume that thoughtful Jane Benson is being thoughtful. Observe. Note what is actually going on before your eyes. *Then* you can draw some conclusions about Bill and Jane and their states of mind and mood.

It's tough to avoid making snap judgments. But make the effort. This exercise in observation not only will make you more perceptive about people. It will have a second effect of the greatest importance to you and your ability to work with people. It will push your awareness of people to a new high. It will make the entire experience of social living, your working and living with people, more vital, fascinating, and creative.

Here's what I mean. When you live in a world of people you don't dig—to use the vernacular—in almost a literal sense you're surrounded by dummies. People seem unexpressive, dull, unstimulating.

However, as your perceptivity increases, you'll find that *people* become more alive. They become not only more understandable when their moods and motives become more obvious to you, but also more predictable. And as the scientist tells us, once we can predict we can control.

The sales manager of a large midwestern distillery recently said, "I know that my top salesman responds poorly to even a temporary slump. As soon as I see his sales figures sliding, I make it a point to get out into the field and spend a few days with him. That way, I've had him in top form for months, even years at a time."

Note the connection between the ability to predict a man's mood and the ability to guide and assist his performance.

III. Look for the things they don't do

Here's a final means of "reading" a person. Watch carefully when you notice that some *expected* action or response is lacking.

In the 14th Century a Spanish writer, Fernando Rojas, wrote a short novel called, "Lazarillo de Tormes." The Lazarillo of the title was a young lad, whose adventures made him as immortal in the culture of Spain as Robin Hood in England or Little Eva in our tradition.

One of the memorable aspects of the Spanish classic are the incidents that reveal human nature in its most basic aspect. For example:

Lazarillo, at the age of eight, becomes the servant of a grasping and cruel blind beggar. The two go about the countryside, the lad leading the beggar about so that he can ply his trade. In one town, the beggar is given a bunch of grapes, which he agrees to share with his poor mistreated servant. It is agreed that each will take a grape at a time, first one, then the other.

In the midst of this process, the blindman gives poor Lazarillo a terrific box on the ear. "Why did you hit me?" protests the lad.

"You're cheating," replies the beggar.

"How can you say that," says the boy. "You can't see me."

"True," says the beggar, "but I know you've been taking more than one grape at a time. I know because I was taking two grapes, and if you hadn't been cheating, you would have protested."

The blind beggar practiced with great skill watching for the thing that *doesn't* happen. "When I got my promotion," a division manager of a chemical company reported, "one of my oldest friends failed to come around and congratulate me. I knew at once that he was deeply upset because he hadn't gotten the job I'd been given."

Double payoff

The better you understand people, the more effectively you can help them. You can take the pressure off a person who tends to wilt when the screws start to turn. You encourage a person who you know loses heart easily. You stimulate a person whose enthusiasm needs assistance from outside to burst into flame.

By using your perceptions about people in ways like these, you build your mastery of them in the most desirable way possible—by increasing your own effectiveness in relation to them. At the same time, you boost their efficiency and their self-satisfaction.

▶ Recap ◀

The highlights of this chapter:

The tool we've been talking about: Your ability to observe and interpret what people are thinking and feeling.

How and when to use it: You apply the tool of "mind reading" when you have to make a judgment about a person, hire him, give him a job assignment or a responsibility. You apply it, also, in your continuing quest to understand the people about you, particularly those you must work with, on the job, at home and in your community. The more perceptive you are about people, the better you can predict their behavior, and the better you can control them.

How to develop the tool: Here are the recommendations that have been made in this chapter:

1. Avoid the standard ineffective ways of judging people: the

generalization, the idea that people are uniform in their behavior, the Grandmother's recipe approach.

2. Use the method of silence to get people to reveal themselves.

3. Forget about yourself, about wanting to make a favorable impression. Concentrate and listen to the other person.

4. Look for five key qualities in a person: tension level, degree of openness, the role he sees for himself in a given situation, the degree of rigidity of thinking, his sense of values.

5. Look for the element of *change*, the departure from normal that tells you something's afoot.

6. Look for the things they *don't* do.

Finally, keep in mind that the *real* objective of this chapter is to make you a more perceptive person. Don't give up if you feel you're not "naturally" a sensitive person. Just as the golfer has to practice and stick with it to become good at the sport, so the ability to perceive and understand people must be acquired piecemeal over a period of time.

You can become as "intuitive" about people as anyone can be. This chapter provides the know-how. Practice using the tool and you'll be able to work wonders with it.

chapter 5

At this point, we've already taken several major strides towards our goal of mastering people. We've covered such crucial elements as making you feel comfortable in the human race, self-understanding —a must for relating successfully to others—how to develop sensitivity to people so that you know where you stand in critical situations.

However, there is one piece to the pattern, important at this stage, that is still missing. Without it, many would-be leaders and managers of people find themselves unaccountably limited. Much to their own surprise, they turn out to be Johnny-One-Notes of the human relations field.

Despite the fact that they've got a great deal going for them, despite their mastery of many of the basic tools, their achievements somehow fall short of their potential. They find themselves clucking when they should be clicking. Why? Because they don't have what it takes to operate successfully *across the board.*

flexibility
— the tool
that makes
everyone
manageable

The power tool that gives you the capacity to work with all kinds of people—young, old, male, female, redheads, blondes and brunettes—is *flexibility*.

The little man who isn't all there

The greatest foe of flexibility in our midst is a creature that looks almost human. See him on the street or in a bus, and you couldn't distinguish him from a normal being. But he's different, somewhat less than he should be. I call him Splinter Man.

Splinter Man is distinguished by a lack of flexibility. He may function well in a few areas, but outside of those, he draws a blank. Here are two typical Splinter Men you may have been exposed to:

A *high school teacher*. He's great with bright students, but simply drags his feet with the lower I.Q. set.

A *supervisor*. He does well with roughnecks, but stumbles badly when he has to deal with people of above average education.

Splinter Man is more to be pitied than blamed. He is what he is because he has been unable to break away from a harmful attitude. Putting it bluntly, Splinter Man is type-minded. Instead of thinking of people as people, *he sees only types*. If a man is in a position of authority, he's Boss. If he's got a job somewhere down the line, why, he's automatically judged as inferior.

The world of Splinter Man is inhabited by poor men, rich men, society people, college graduates, factory workers, secretaries, housewives, salesmen. Never, but never are people just plain human beings, individuals, a Molly Jones or a Henry Smith.

Splinter Man's way of thinking means that he sees people through mental blinders. Consider the serious problems he faces in dealing with people:

He can't accept the fact that a man may be uneducated, but may be intellectually brilliant.

He can't understand that a man might be highly educated, but be a dull, unimaginative, stupid bore.

He can't believe that a woman might be a housewife, but be interested in problems outside her home and community.

How Splinter Man loses out

Want to see how a man without flexibility messes up the works? A gag that had them in stitches on Madison Avenue makes a good case in point. Here's how a Splinter Man would handle an interview with a job applicant:

The scene is an advertising office. A young man trying for a copywriter's job is talking to the agency interviewer—really a Splinter Man in disguise:

Splinter Man: Had experience writing copy for cigarettes?
Job Applicant: Yes.
Splinter Man: Kingsize?
Job Applicant: Yes.
Splinter Man: Filter tip?
Job Applicant: Yes.
Splinter Man: With menthol?
Job Applicant: Uh—no . . .
Splinter Man: Sorry, we can't use you.

See what's happened? To those with Splinter-Man tendencies, people must fit into pigeonholes or they're out. And it would be tough to say who loses more.

Scientists have a word for it

If this rigid ineffectual way of regarding people were limited to Splinter Men—fortunately, there aren't too many of them around—the harm would be relatively slight. But psychologists tell us that the tendency which Splinter Man exemplifies in the extreme, is distributed to a greater or lesser degree among most of us.

Dr. David Emery, well-known industrial psychologist, states, "Stereotypy, the tendency to form mental stereotypes, is a well-recognized mental aberration whose occurrence is more widespread than is generally suspected."

It's the person suffering from stereotypy who accepts the following statements as gospel:

All redheads are hotheads.
You shouldn't trust a man who can't look you in the eye.
Looseness in women is betrayed by heavy use of make-up.
Men with small chins are weaklings and cowards.

What Splinter Man and those who suffer from his problem lack is *flexibility of outlook*. Accordingly, they are hampered at almost every turn in their human relations dealings. They find it hard to accept the new and different. Any change leaves them hanging on the ropes. To simply say, "They are set in their ways," is likely to be a gross understatement. Notice the difficulty inflexible individuals suffer in their dealings with people:

. . . *job relationships*. Splinter Man is thrown for a loss almost every time a stranger appears on the horizon. For example, one of the breed suffered particularly great hardships when a new boss took over his department. "I got along swell with Mr. Ederle," Ken Boardman tells his wife, "because he was a positive person who always knew his mind. But my new boss is so wishy-washy, I just don't know how to deal with him."

Granted that it's easier to work under a superior who knows exactly what he wants and how he wants it. The fact remains that many bosses aren't like that. By developing a flexible approach, we can make our working lives a lot happier and successful by adjusting to whatever boss we happen to inherit with our jobs.

. . . *living situations*. "I'm used to small town life," Mrs. James tells her husband tearfully, "and small town people. These sophisticated suburbanites just aren't for me. You'll just have to give up your new job . . ."

We all feel sorry for Mrs. James. It's completely understandable that a person who finds small town life congenial might find it difficult going in the suburbs of a big city. But Mrs. James, a Splinter Woman, has needlessly set her mind to a particular pattern that is stifling her ability to enjoy life and people. She is also, and not by coincidence, standing in the way of her husband's career.

The fact is, most of us are endowed with the capacity for flexibility at birth. It's a quality we inherit from an early ancestor. Here's the background.

Your flexible forebears

Your family tree may not boast an Uncle Pete, but go back about seven million years, and scientists will tell you you had an ancestor named *Dryopithecus*.

This early relative was quite a guy. To his way of thinking, trees were for the birds, and he took up residence on the ground, where food was more abundant. This early-model human changed his ways in still another direction. Unlike George Bernard Shaw, he felt that vegetables by themselves made for a dull diet. Accordingly, he stretched his menu to include chops and steaks along with the carrots and peas.

Most important of all, *Dryopithecus* was able to catch on to the trick of using stones or a rude club for felling his food—early proof of the efficacy of the tool concept. At the same time, he used pear-shaped grunts as a sort of rudimentary speech. Here was a vocal boy who made good.

An early loser

On the other hand, take *Tyrannosaurus Rex*, a dinosaur that lived some 250 million years ago. He stood about 20 feet high and measured 45 feet from head to tail. Thick, armored hide shielded his vital organs. Three sharp claws at the end of his forelimbs had the bite of a steam-shovel. He could have licked a couple of dozen *Dryopithecusses* with one limb tied behind his tail.

The only thing the *Tyrannosaurus* couldn't do was change. Scientists tell us that this one weakness accounted for his relatively short existence on earth. Small drops in temperature, to which he couldn't adapt himself, led to his eventual destruction.

Why we survived

Dryopithecus had one vital quality: he could change his habits to suit the conditions in which he found himself. And this ability he passed along to us, his descendants.

When the weather turned cold, for example, early man covered himself with warm furry hides. Eventually, he learned, by using fire, to provide himself with both light and heat.

The quality of flexibility, the capacity to adapt to change, is still rated among our most important assets. And, as we stated earlier, this tool of flexibility is essential for you to work successfully with all kinds of people.

The extent to which we personally possess this quality plays an important part in our day to day dealings with people. If we're flexible, for example, we ride the bumps in human relationships more successfully; a falling out with a colleague becomes merely an incident that is soon healed over; a new boss, new neighbors, or new job associates become easier to take.

Psychologists have spent a good deal of time measuring this quality which often decides whether we can make the most of our opportunities. Here's your chance to see to what extent you possess this capability.

Test your flexibility

To measure the extent to which you have this important quality, just answer the questions below as accurately as possible. The franker you are, the more meaningful your score will be. When you've gone through all 12 questions, rate yourself according to the directions at the end of the quiz.

	Yes	No
1. Do you think pretty girls are generally stupid?	___	___
2. You meet a stranger who tells you he can communicate with others by means of thought waves. Would you feel he is nutty?	___	___
3. Do you feel a man who avoids looking you in the eye can be trusted?	___	___
4. Do you generally disagree with the idea that "What was good enough for me is good enough for my kids?"	___	___
5. When you have to stay out overnight, do you find it difficult to fall asleep in a strange bed?	___	___
6. Do you have a strong preference for members of the opposite sex with a definite kind of appearance—tall, dark and handsome males, for example, or red-headed females?	___	___
7. You're the parent of an eleven year old. It's a standard part of summer outings to go hiking up a		

                                                    Yes   No

mountain trail, you leading the way. This year the
youngster asks "to go first." Are you pleased?   ____ ____
8. Do you generally prefer this year's styles—in clothing or cars—to last year's?   ____ ____
9. Are you annoyed by the fact that some men wear
   toupees?   ____ ____
10. If you were the husband of a woman who wanted
    to dye her hair, would it be okay with you?   ____ ____
11. If you were the wife of a man who didn't want to
    "keep up with the Jones's," would you be annoyed
    with him for it?   ____ ____
12. Answer the following questions as rapidly as you
    can:
    (a) How many ends does a pencil have?   ____
    (b) Two pencils?   ____
    (c) Two-and-a-half pencils?   ____

Give yourself 10 points for each question answered correctly:

1. No; 2. No; 3. Yes; 4. Yes; 5. No; 6. No; 7. Yes; 8. Yes; 9. No; 10. Yes;
11. No; 12. (a) 2; (b) 4; (c) 6.

It's your answer to (c) that counts. If you had 6, give yourself 10
points. Half a pencil, of course, has as many ends as a whole one.
Now rate yourself by the following scale:
100–120 Good and flexible
 70–90 You'll bend if you must
 40–60 Odds are, you won't make it
  0–30 Stiff as a board

How to develop your flexibility

How did you make out in the quiz? Maybe you're pleased with your
score, maybe not. But one way or the other, it's important to remember
that flexibility in dealing with people is a tool you can sharpen.

Best bet to boost your flexibility is to keep practicing simple exercises. Actually, it's possible to take a lot of the stiffness out of your
outlook. Here are a few brief tips that will help increase your flexibility:

. . . don't be afraid to question "facts" about people. Often they're
just opinions in camouflage.

. . . recognize that there can often be more than one "right"
person for an assignment or job.

. . . when you disagree with someone, try, really try, to understand his point of view.

. . . re-examine your own views about the people you know, every once in a while. Watch for the danger signals in a sentence beginning, "I've always thought that Frank . . ." You may be surprised to find that your ideas about Frank are more rigid than they should be.

Remember that the odds are in your favor, since being human means that you have a certain amount of flexibility built right into your personality. It's one of the unique qualities that sets us above the animal kingdom, and explains why we ride horses instead of vice versa.

Now, to concentrate more heavily on flexibility-building, here are some major steps.

Guidelines: four steps to increased flexibility

1. *Accept the variety of people.* President John F. Kennedy, during his European visit in June, 1963, asked his audiences to help "make the world safe for diversity." The world *is* diverse, politically, nationally, socially—and, of course, in its many peoples.

Accept the variety of people—both in the large sense, and in the sense close to home—among your fellow citizens, colleagues, and so on. We humans come in all shapes, sizes and dispositions. We're tall and short, wise and less so, male and female, old and young, genteel and boorish, bold and shy. Do we have to like all these people equally? No, of course not. But this doesn't mean that we need reject the types of people we personally find hard to take, which takes us to our second point:

2. *Distinguish between what you like in people and what you accept.* "I find it easier to get along with people of good breeding," protests Splinter Man. That's an honest statement. But it doesn't necessarily follow that Splinter Man should therefore avoid all association with the less well bred. As the confirmed user of flexibility knows, every type of person has his interest and worth. For example, the less well educated person often has an originality and spontaneity that sometimes gets educated out of many of his fellow humans.

It may be natural to have preferences, to like blondes better than brunettes, to prefer athletes to bookworms (or vice versa), to develop a lively passion for unusual people, in comparison to the more conforming ones. But this does not mean, and shouldn't mean, that you therefore stick with the people you prefer and scorn everyone else. Remember, your objective is to manage all people. And to do so successfully, you must mingle with and respect all kinds.

3. *Practice rut-busting daily.* Psychologists speak of a person's "set," a predisposition toward standard situations. Set keeps one going through the same routines, day in, day out. You sharpen your flexibility by making it a point to break out of your routine as often as possible. Are the consequences of rut-busting dire? Painful? On the contrary!

A friend of mine is a born Manhattanite, urbane, sophisticated— yet one of the most limited people I know. One day I decided that he needed a little *flexibilizing.*

I phoned him one pleasant spring morning and said, "Clem, I'll be down at your apartment in 15 minutes. I'm taking you on a trip," and hung up before he could ask a lot of silly questions.

An hour later we were in the town of Haverstraw, New York, visiting a state-run rehabilitation hospital, talking to the doctors, therapists, case workers, and the patients themselves. It was an illuminating experience, a rare view of people suffering from all kinds of physical handicaps, coping with their problems in heroic style.

When I delivered him back to his apartment, my friend was almost visibly transformed. "You know," he confided, "I haven't been as moved, or stimulated, or *educated* by anything in years."

Make it a point to *flexibilize* yourself as frequently as possible. Do the unusual and different to broaden your contacts with people. Within reason, of course. There is no intention here to suggest the hazardous or the unpleasant. But make an effort to break through the routines of your normal activity. No matter where you stand on the social ladder, there is bound to be a ladder full of people to explore. See for yourself how the other half lives:

Do you go to the "same old place" every vacation time? Try a change of pace—another area, another type of facility. New places mean new people, individuals of different tastes and values.

Restaurants? Most communities offer quite an array. If you now go to "the best one in town," try another. Even if the experience simply ends up with your appreciating your favorite all the more, the change will have been worthwhile. Again you'll see new faces, new approaches to living, different types of human behavior.

Do you spend all your time with "the old crowd"? How about

someone different? How about the new man or woman in the office, or the one who's moved in next door?

4. *Above all, use flexibility in your dealings with people.* You've read about Ken Boardman, and his boss trouble. If Ken used a flexible approach to people, he wouldn't have a problem.

Make it a point to break down the barriers of your thinking about people. Approach them freely, openly, with as few preconceptions as possible. Let them prove themselves, show what they are. Don't prejudge, don't fog your view of them with assumptions.

Furthermore, don't develop a "my kind of people" complex. Don't think—or if you do, modify your thinking—that, "He's the only kind of boss I can work with." Or, if you're in a supervisory or executive position, "He's the kind of subordinate I can get along with."

Flexibility can become a master tool for managing your affairs with people if you set up a goal of openmindedness and respect for all. Sure, some people are better, brighter, more attractive, easier to deal with than others. But learn how to deal with everyone, every type, age and disposition.

Another positive point in your flexible approach: Remember, when you were a youngster, there was a good deal of talk about developing a "line" or special manner in your approach to the opposite sex? Well, don't use the "line," or pre-packaged approach to people. Let the situation determine what you say, and how you say it. Be sincere, be spontaneous. Let your flexibility help you work wonders with people as you accept them, treat them with respect, look for the worthy aspects of their being.

And now for a final idea that can clinch your use of flexibility.

The pygmalion technique

George Bernard Shaw wrote a play called "Pygmalion," which has been made into the most successful musical of all time—"My Fair Lady." The essence of the story is that a certain Professor Higgins, a language expert, takes Eliza Doolittle, a girl of the streets, and transforms her into a great social success by teaching her to speak English properly.

Although the point is not explicitly made, it is clear that the artful professor has the ability to look at a ragged, dirty-faced, sniveling flower girl, and imagine the difference that a bath and a liberal dose of improved English could make.

This ability to look at people, and perceive them not only as they are, *but as they might be*—with specific attributes added or taken away—is an especially effective way to flexibilize your view of people. It helps you see people not only as they are, but as they *can* be—after training, after they've had experience on the firing line, education, even how they'd look with different grooming.

Elizabeth T. Murner, an executive in a midwestern employment agency told me: "I had a young girl come in about a top secretarial job. Her appearance would have killed her chances. I suggested that she go out and get her hair cut short and change into a simpler style of dress. She did as I suggested and she got the job."

Thomas Janeway, president of the Janeway Canning Company of Buffalo, has developed the pygmalion technique, this flexible way of seeing people, to a fine art. He uses it particularly in hiring and promoting his people. Says Mr. Janeway, "When I'm confronted by a job applicant, or considering a man for advancement, I think of him in terms of his future achievement. What impression will this callow lad make in two or three years, after he's had some of the rough edges polished off? How will that young man shape up after he's been out selling and learned to stand up in a tough, competitive field?"

Use the pygmalion technique to broaden your view of people. You do it by mentally throwing your view of a person slightly out of focus, adding or subtracting particular qualities. You might then say:

"If Ed Carnes learned to read blueprints, he'd be a good prospect for the supervisory staff."

"If Helen Miller took a sketching course, she'd make a darned good assistant art director."

Notice the effect of the pygmalion technique. It puts you in a position to help people improve themselves, to acquire background, experience or specific training that can make them more valuable to themselves and to you. *This is management of people in its most constructive guise.*

Don't try to outdo God

Another rule to help sharpen your use of flexibility as a tool: avoid classifying people as "good" and "bad." That's all right for Western movies or children's fairy tales. But in real life, we seldom find individuals quite as cut-and-dried. As Joaquin Miller, the American poet, put it:

In men whom men pronounce as ill, I find so much goodness still. In men whom men pronounce divine, I find so much sin and blot; I hesitate to draw the line between the two, when God has not.

And learn from these various people, in all their many ways. This doesn't mean adopt the views and values of others, helter-skelter. Try to understand the way they see things, their scale of values, what makes them tick.

Once you apply this tool of flexibility to your human relations, you'll find you begin to develop an edge that works very much in your favor. You'll come to be known as the person who can "deal with any-one," or a person who can "supervise all kinds of people." Doors of opportunity will suddenly open up to you as this major asset of success-ful leadership becomes yours.

▶ Recap ◀

Just to make sure you're not overlooking any bets, here's a run-through of the key points in this chapter:

The tool: flexibility.

When to use it: in your judgments and attitudes towards people, on and off the job.

Use it particularly to take the threat out of new faces and new situations involving people. New employees in your company, new neighbors, can mean greater opportunity for you *if* you use the tool of flexibility and convert a threat brought on by aloofness or hostility to a happy promise by open and understanding acceptance.

How to develop it: the suggestions spelled out for you are summed up in four key points:

1. Accept the variety of people.
2. Distinguish between what you like in people, and what you accept.
3. Practice rut-busting daily.
4. Use flexibility in your dealings with people—all people.

Finally, practice the pygmalion technique. Use it to broaden your view of people, to improve your perspective on their potentialities and to make them more valuable to themselves and to you.

Part II

Increase Your Influence and Control

chapter 6

"O.K., Jerry," says young Al Mayes, "see if you and the rest can do better on the next cycle."

But despite the foreman's plea, the group *doesn't* do better next time around. They do worse! And it takes a call by novice Mayes to veteran Fred Wladyka, ex-head of the group, to straighten out the mess. You'll soon learn the whole case history, including an explanation of why Al Mayes failed to get anywhere with his crew.

what you must know to master people in groups

People in groups —a special problem

With this chapter we enter a new area of challenge and opportunity—the mastery of people *in groups*. Much of our dealings with people takes place within the framework of an organization:

. . . on the job, we work in group situations—the company, department, or committee.

. . . On the home front, we're involved in all kinds of groups—fraternal, civic, church, sports. Name an activity, and it's almost sure to involve a group or organization.

The business world has developed a keen awareness of the importance of the group to industry. Says Charles Kolker, top executive of a New Jersey chemical company, "Today, teamwork is the key to advances on many fronts. The solitary grandstander is a thing of the past. The small work unit, the research team, the task force are the established tools for tackling specific targets. Group action, group efficiency and group leadership—these are the means for getting results, today and tomorrow."

It is agreed, then, that a major aspect of mastery of people gets you into the area of group control. The trouble is that working with groups can be a shadowy, fog-bound activity. And to some people, scared by the problems of handling individuals, the idea of coping with *masses* of people seems almost hopeless.

But relax! Later on in the chapter, you'll find spelled out the guidelines you need to take you behind the scenes of group organization, group moods, group reactions. Specific recommendations will reveal to you how to read the signs of group behavior.

With this hard information in your grasp, you can cut the problems of group control down to size. You'll be able to pursue the goals you set for yourself in group mastery—whether it's that of leader, or of a center of influence and power that can swing the group to your point of view.

What you *won't* find in these pages is the old-fashioned approach to group leadership exemplified by the drill sergeant and the "bull-of-the-woods" type of supervisor.

Many years ago, all it took to warn us of an approaching enemy was a Paul Revere, and a simple one-if-by-land, two-if-by-sea routine. Today, it takes a string of electronic stations comprising the Distant Early Warning system. Similarly, today's needs require more than a loud bellow and a show of muscle to get top performance from a group of people. Above all else, it takes a knowledge of just what a group is, what makes it different from a simple aggregation of individuals, and the leader's ability to read the group mind. This is the approach you'll find in the pages ahead.

A good assumption to avoid

Here's rule No. 1: Don't go on the assumption that a group behaves just like an individual. The experts in human behavior know that there's a unique quality about a group. For example, psychologists are aware that people in groups, because of the interaction among them, develop attitudes and behavior they never would have as individuals.

Just think of the phrase "mob rule." We know of historic instances where crowds of people, whipped to a frenzy by rabble-rousing tactics, have burned and pillaged and killed. And when the carnage was over, individuals examined their gruesome handiwork in horrified anguish, asking themselves, "How could I have done such a thing?"

The answer is, they did them because of group dynamics—the forces and pressures that are created within groups. Many experiments have been performed that show what happens to people in group situations that makes them respond unexpectedly. One of the most dramatic was conducted by the famous experimental psychologist Muzafer Sherif. His aim was to show how group pressures affect individuals in their *power to observe* and in their *judgments*.

How group forces change the individual

Sherif's study showed in a specific manner how a group forces its members to develop a group standard that displaces individual views. Here's what Dr. Sherif did.

He started with the fact that a small fixed point of light, flashed briefly in darkness, will *seem* to move. Different people see the apparent movement differently.

Sherif first asked a number of people, individually, to tell how far the light seemed to jump. These judgments proved to be more or less consistent for each person.

Then the setup was changed. The same test was given to the same people, but now *several took the test together*. Each individual heard the responses given by others in the group. When called on to judge the movement under these conditions, the judgments tended to converge! The group responses were much closer to one another than the individual responses had been. *In effect, a group standard had been formed.*

In other words, what had happened was this: if A had originally thought the light shifted two inches, and he heard B say the light jumped only one inch, A would shade his answer somewhat and say that the light had jumped an inch and a half. And B, for the same reason, would tend to shade *his* observation, making it closer to A's and he would say the light jumped "about an inch and a half," although when on his own he had estimated the movement at one inch. This one example makes the point: people in groups influence one another and thereby develop unique attitudes and standards.

A typical group in action

Now see how group unity can kick back when the leader doesn't know his stuff and becomes a *victim* of group power rather than the power that leads the group.

When I was a member of management in the Plastics Division of the Celanese Corporation of America, I had the occasion to see many examples of group leadership—both good and bad. I particularly recall the case of a young supervisor who had just been put in charge of a forming crew. Because he lacked the skills of group control, his men gave him a rough time. Eventually, he learned the ropes, ended up as one of the best foremen in the entire plant. But the case history you're about to read catches him at the rocky start of his supervisory career . . .

Out of control

Tension . . . It was evident in the strident tones of the young foreman as he talked over the phone. "Fred, you'd better get over here. Every sheet the men have formed in the last hour is a reject."

The Sheet-Forming Division of the Celanese Corporation's Plastics plant in Newark was the scene, Al Mayes the supervisor who was in trouble. Calling the ex-head of the department had been a bitter pill for him to swallow. It was an admission that after three weeks in his new job, he faced a situation he couldn't handle.

Five minutes later a car wheeled onto the gravel of the outside yard.

Fred Wladyka strode in and walked over to the inspection tables, where the girls had the formed sheets set out. Al Mayes joined him. "Orange peel," he said, pointing to the stippling that ruined the optical quality of the clear acetate sheets.

"Heat's too low," Fred said.

Through all this, the six men of the forming crew continued working, as though unmindful of the two foremen. But even young Al Mayes knew their behavior was just a little too casual, too studied. They knew darn well what was going on.

Wladyka headed for the heating ovens, where the men stood. "Hi," he said, and got a mixture of non-committal greetings in return. "You fellows lost your touch?" he kidded. "You haven't made a good one in the last hour."

"It's the material," Joe Rustani said.

"O.K.," the veteran foreman replied. "Let's make some good pieces out of bad material, then. Hank," to one of the crew, "push that thermostat up to 450 degrees. Set the timer at a minute more than you've been running."

The directions were followed. The timer rang, the two oven men opened the long door and slid the rack out that held the heat-softened plastic, and it was spread over a triangular wooden form. The entire crew slowly pulled the sheet, stretching it till the limit marks at the bottom of the form were reached.

"Looks good," Wladyka said. Al Mayes joined him, and after a few minutes, when the sheet had set, he stripped it off the form and held it up to the light.

"Best glider window we've ever turned out," he said. Then to the crew, "O.K., men, you can break for lunch."

After the room had cleared out, Wladyka looked at the young foreman quizzically. "They've been giving you a hard time."

"They sure have. I thought I knew how to work with people. When I was a leadman in the chopout room, I never had any trouble with my two-man crew. But a group this size—it's just a different animal."

The mystery of group leadership

There are several noteworthy aspects to the thumbnail case history just cited. For example, note these:

1. *The subtle nature of group resistance.* It's a lesson the Nazis

learned during World War II. Subjugated populations in Denmark, Holland, France, on the surface obediently followed the regulations laid down by the occupation authorities. But in addition to underground resistance, citizens dragged their feet, thwarted the so-called master race in a dozen different ways.

That's why Al Mayes was stopped cold. If the men had bucked him in open rebellion, he might have been able to overcome their resistance. But against the below-surface hostility, he was helpless.

Watch for this in your own group situations. Don't assume just because no one comes right out and objects to what you're trying to do, that they're going along. It's only when the group *acts*, backs you up by a vote or actually pitches in to follow your wishes, that you know they're pulling with you and for you.

2. *The importance of picking the right "transmitter."* If you'll check back, you'll see that when Al Mayes addressed his orders to the group, he picked Jerry as the individual to aim them at. But Fred Wladyka picked Hank.

Both Jerry and Hank were being used as transmission belts, to transmit instructions to the forming crew. But Al Mayes hadn't yet learned that it was Hank who was the informal leader of the group, *not* Jerry. And it was in part his violation of group protocol that had gotten the group's back up. You'll find more on the important matter of informal leaders in the next few pages.

3. *The need to assert authority properly.* You probably detected a difference in the way the young foreman approached his group as compared to the veteran's manner. With more experience, Al Mayes was able to do as Fred Wladyka did—assert the power of his authority so as to get complete obedience.

The proper use of authority is a surefire key to group control. If you're in a position of authority—on the job, because you're a supervisor or executive, in civic affairs because you're an elected officer— you must understand that the authority you've been given is the rock on which your group mastery depends.

This doesn't mean you throw your weight around or that you back up every order with a show of authority. It does mean that you're aware of the ultimate form your authority may take. For example:

On the job, a supervisor has the power to reprimand a disobedient employee, warn him of the consequences of his continued disobedience and finally, may even transfer or fire a man in extreme cases.

In a social or sports group, the leader can apply his power merely by asserting it: "You elected me coach of the team, and what I say goes." Or, in some cases, it can be done by bringing group pressure to bear on an upstart: "Fellow members, one person in our group refuses to join in our clean-up campaign and that means he's spoiling things for all of us . . ."

Group mindreading made easy

Knowing about the informal leadership of a group, the interaction between members of the group, the clues to look for that tell you what the group is thinking and feeling, these are the crucial keys to group control. Now here are the specific facts and ideas you need in these critical areas to build your ability to get groups on your side, working the way you want them to, towards objectives that you select.

I. The five clues to group mood

When you speak of an individual's mood, there's no mystery about what you mean. A happy man smiles, has a lift to his gait and his voice usually reflects lightness in tone, selection of words and so on. The angry man signals his mood by the expression on his face, speaking from between clenched teeth and so on.

When you're dealing with people in groups, the signs are also there —but *they're considerably tougher to detect.* You have to know what to look for to get an accurate reading of the group temper. Here are five checkpoints that tell you what's going on below the surface. Using them, you can read the group mind as easily and unerringly as if the facts were printed in black and white:

A. Workpace

"I couldn't figure out what had gotten into my staff," an office manager told me recently. "A week ago I came in and found my gang working away like all get out. At first I was mighty pleased. But when it went on for two days, I began to worry.

"Finally I asked the head bookkeeper, one of my oldtimers. Guess what I learned? There was a rumor going around that we were going to bring in automatic equipment that was going to mean a layoff of 50% of the department. I guess everyone was scared and trying to make a good showing."

Any change in the workpace usually indicates something is afoot. In the case described above, worry was causing an accelerated pace. But undoubtedly you've seen cases where a lagging workpace meant group frustration or rebellion.

Just remember, pace is basic. The pace at which a group does its work ties in with the very core of its mood.

What you look for specifically are *changes* of workpace. The secret is to be able to distinguish between normal changes and those that signal all's not well.

Sometimes, of course, an altered pace can be explained by an obvious fact. If the tempo picks up under the pressure of a deadline there's no need to look for a "hidden message."

But when there is a change you cannot explain right off the bat, check either through direct questions or examining background events. For example, if you know that your company has just cracked down on extra rest periods, the answer is as simple as putting two and two together.

B. Response to orders

Eric Graham, director of a little theater group in Queens recently faced a crisis. His group was rehearsing "The Seven-Year Itch," the George Axelrod comedy about a husband who tries to make time while his wife's away in the country.

Graham was telling the leading man how he was supposed to act when the charming blonde from upstairs first appears on his doorstep.

"I don't see it that way," the actor said. Then he began a rambling —and to Eric Graham—cockeyed analysis of the action.

The director rightly interpreted the actor's argument as a sign of resistance to his authority. He nipped the revolt in the bud by saying, "I'm sorry, but I've given this part a great deal of study and thought. Since I'm the director, we'll do it my way. O.K.?"

Although Graham hadn't put it into words, the next sign of refusal from the actor would have met with, "If you don't see it the way I do, I'll just have to get another actor for the part."

The actor got the message and went along. The entire group, which had watched the brief struggle with extreme interest, also got the message. Everybody settled down, and the rehearsal proceeded in good order.

In your own situation—whether you're dealing with your family, a group at the office or a committee in one of your community organizations—note the manner in which your orders are received.

This doesn't mean that if they obey, everything is great and if they argue you're in trouble. That's a dangerous oversimplification. You can get disagreement in a cooperative way. For example, a member of the group may take issue with a minor detail:

"I think the newsletter is a great idea," one of your committee members may say, "but wouldn't it be better if we timed the mailing so that it doesn't get lost in the Christmas rush?"

By the same token, agreement that represents meek obedience may be undesirable.

You tell the desirable from the undesirable response to your instructions by the tone or manner of the response. Where the spirit is cooperative, you're in the clear. But if the group drags its feet, responds meekly and unenthusiastically, then the group mood is working against you and you'd better dig to find out what's at the bottom of the discontent.

There's no question about how you learn what's what. You ask. For example:

"Tom, I have the feeling that although I didn't get any argument on my request, you're not wholeheartedly in favor of the action. Do you have any doubts?"

C. Seesawing—the difference between watched and unwatched behavior

It's only natural for people to make a point of looking busy when the boss is around. On the other hand, the would-be leader who notices a big difference between his people's efforts when he's in sight and when he's away has a problem.

The fact is if your presence *either* boosts or blocks productive effort, it's a sign of trouble. Behind this type of situation can be found:

. . . *misunderstanding.* They may feel you respond favorably to apple-polishing, and so they put on a show for your benefit.

. . . *overcompetitiveness.* Certain individuals may think the way to make a good impression is to show up the other fellow in your presence. Which one or combination of the above you face doesn't make too much difference. What does matter is that you try to find out what's at the bottom of their behavior. You do it by (a) talking directly with your people; (b) a quick review of recent developments in the group.

D. Do they walk that extra mile?

"We have a wonderful church group," a lady recently told me. "Whenever the word goes out that we're having a church supper, people *call me* to ask what they can do."

This is a *creative* response. When the group that you're working with anticipates what's needed, is eager to help, volunteers for extra duty, especially when there's no material compensation, you can be sure that morale is high and almost any action that you plan for the group will get full cooperation.

I use the word "creative" to describe this group attitude because it emphasizes the *quality* rather than the quantity of the group's reaction.

When people are willing to take the time and trouble to devote their creative energies to doing what you want them to do, to advance group goals, you're riding high—and so are they.

E. Psychological fringe behavior can signal deep trouble

The American Telephone and Telegraph Company recently faced an unusual problem. The washrooms of one of their offices were being marred by obscene words and pictures scrawled all over the walls. But AT&T's efforts to cope with the problem ran into a snag. The thought had been to photograph the person or persons responsible. But employees found the hidden automatic camera, and demanded that it be removed. The company acceded—but was still left with the unsolved problem.

The probability is that AT&T executives were less upset by the physical damage to company facilities than by the intimations of unrest in the employee group.

There are many clues that groups can give you to indicate that all's not well. Destruction or misuse of physical facilities is one symptom. Thoughtless horseplay, the need to "blow off steam" means that pressures are building up.

The interesting thing about this type of destructive "fringe be-havior" is that it usually involves a small clique. Within the group, only two or three trouble makers may be involved in this undesirable fringe behavior. When you spot the trouble makers, you can use one of two approaches:

. . . *lay it on the line with them.* Let them know that they're in a small minority, that they're not acting in the interests of the group and that you want their undesirable activities to cease.

. . . *isolate them or separate them, if possible.* This alternative suggests that you may have to crack down. Since their behavior is creating a problem, make it clear that you feel that in the interests of the majority, you are requesting them, if they cannot mend their ways, to separate from the group.

2. Look for interaction among group members for the shape of things to come

It happened in a small town near Buffalo, New York. As John Wakefield sat on his porch, two neighbors walked by, chatting to one another. Wakefield called to his wife, "Things are going to be a lot pleasanter around here from now on."

"Why, John?"

"Tim Owens and Bill Redler just walked by together."

To an outsider that single observation might seem to make little sense. But Wakefield could explain it simply. Tim and Bill are heads of two rival factions in the neighborhood. There'd been ill feeling between them for some time. But if the new friendliness between them lasts, the feud is over.

The manner in which members of your group interact with one another is a dead giveaway to the emotional climate that's brewing. Here's another example:

The cross-check technique

A veteran plant executive of a print shop in Washington, D. C., told me of one method he uses to check group mood. He compares two employees' reactions to an assignment given one of them. To do this he uses a chart, a simple visual device that makes it easy to make the comparison. For example:

Joe Jones is given the task of cleaning up a machine, preparatory to putting it back in production.

Sam Smith, a co-worker of Joe's is frequently as interested in Joe's assignments as Joe himself.

Spelled out in four charts below are some of the possible situations revealed when you compare Joe's and Sam's approval or disapproval of Joe's assignment. You may want to write in some of the additional possibilities.

JOE JONES' ASSIGNMENT

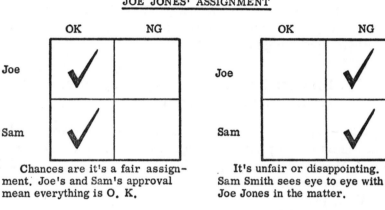

Chances are it's a fair assignment. Joe's and Sam's approval mean everything is O. K.

Other possibilities? _____
_____
_____

It's unfair or disappointing. Sam Smith sees eye to eye with Joe Jones in the matter.

Other possibilities? _____
_____
_____

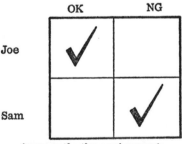

Apparently the assignment pleases Joe. Sam's reaction may be based on envy or resentment.

Other possibilities? _____
_____
_____

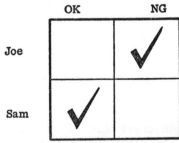

Sam Smith does not like the assignment; is therefore pleased to see Joe get it.

Other possibilities? _____
_____
_____

In general, by noting the relationships among the attitudes expressed by various individuals, you can get a good idea of:

. . . the *amount of tension* that exists between individual members of your group. This can tell you whether past judgments of yours involving two or more individuals have actually been accepted, or are still resented.

. . . the *feelings between sub-groups, or cliques.* This can tell you whether the existence of cliques in your department is good, bad or has reached the stage where you've got to step in.

. . . the extent to which your people *pattern their ideas after others.* With this information at hand, you know the key people to reach in order to get the quickest spread of information or an idea. There are your informal leaders, your group "influentials", whom you can use to transmit your ideas and policies to the group.

Six key questions help you read your group's mind

So far, we've developed a number of methods for reading the group mind. Here's a set of questions that helps you delve even deeper.

If you know the answers to the six questions below you have major clues to important group relationships:

Who likes to *work with* whom? (And which of your people steer clear of joint assignments?)

Who is *often seen together* with whom? (And who of your group avoid one another?)

Who usually *talks to whom?* (And which ones aren't speaking?)

Who *makes suggestions* to whom? (And who takes the attitude, "Let him find out for himself?")

Who *accepts suggestions* from whom? (And who would "rather be wrong in his own way than right in X's?")

Who *is friendly with* whom? (And who wouldn't touch whom with a ten-foot pole?)

Stumped by any of them? You can learn the answers by observing your group's actions.

3. Distinguish between the formal and informal group

Several times in this chapter, we've talked about sub-groups or cliques. This brings up a key finding that group psychologists have been investigating and discussing for years. This is the idea of the *informal group structure,* and *informal leaders.*

When scientists speak of the informal group, they're talking about the clique, the small group within a group that is found both on the work scene and off.

Almost every group has an "informal structure." It's as true of church congregations as it is of a departmental roster in an office or factory. The informal structure shows up in personal relationships— the influentials, the individuals who are looked up to by their fellows as "natural leaders."

The informal leader

The mere existence of an informal leader within a group may signify a number of things—some desirable, some undesirable. It may indicate that there's a division of interest within the group. There may, for example, be a "liberal versus a conservative" division, or, on the work scene, there may be a division between the "let's get away with as little work as possible" group and the more serious-minded group that feels it owes a certain amount of loyalty and effort to an employer that's paying their way.

Regardless of the exact makeup or purposes of the informal group, it's important for you to know who the informal leader or leaders are.

Generally these leaders are the "influentials." They're the ones you can work through to help put over a project, to gain backing for a policy, to enforce discipline.

Of course you have to watch it very carefully. It's perfectly all right for you to use informal leaders to work with you, to try to win their backing as a means of getting broader cooperation from the group. What you must *never* do is abdicate your responsibilities and let the informal leaders take over.

It's in the knowing use of your authority that you make it plain to the group as a whole that you are the man in authority, the man to be obeyed regardless of the informal leadership that may exist.

Another key point: Don't try to lock horns with the informal leader. There's nothing wrong with his hold on group respect, even allegiance, as long as he doesn't misuse his power. Generally you'll get much further by having him work with you than trying to neutralize his hold on his own private clique.

One particularly valuable use of the informal leader is that he can help you sound out potential group reactions to an idea or a program. You don't have to poll the entire group. A chat with informal leader A and informal leader B and you can know pretty well what the reaction would be to the plan for a group picnic, a new work program, and so on.

▶ RECAP ◀

To pick up the key points in this chapter, just run through the lines below:

The tool we've been talking about: group control.

When to use it: when the people you're working with belong to a department, club, team, committee, task force and so on.

How to develop it: First, remember these three principles:

. . . don't make the assumption that a group behaves like a single person. It's because group behavior is a thing by itself that there's a sub-science known as group psychology.

. . . learn to use rather than fight the informal leader.

. . . use authority sparingly, but effectively, when the situation demands it.

In addition, take advantage of these guidelines:

1. Watch for the five clues to group mood.

2. Look for the interaction among group members to learn what's ahead in group "weather" or "climate."

3. When you want to pin down the specifics of group relationships, use the six key questions on page 83.

4. Distinguish between the formal and informal group structure, use the informal leader to help you click with the group.

chapter 7

In Chapter 4 we talked about developing your perceptivity to people. As you remember, we discussed the ways and means of assessing their secret moods and feelings. Now we're going to develop another tool for piercing the barrier that people —either consciously or unconsciously—erect around themselves. This is a specialized single-purpose tool, designed for the single but important purpose of *getting the truth*.

That beautiful word *truth* is very deceptive. It sounds so simple, so solid, "Just tell me the truth," a parent begs a child. "Tell me what actually happened," a policeman asks a motorist involved in an accident.

And what do we find? Despite the child's best intentions, his sense of reality isn't sufficiently developed to tell the truth. And accordingly, the parent is given a child's vivid fantasy:

"A big teddy bear with a green tail came in during the night and broke my rocking horse," the child answers.

**how to
get people
to level
with you**

"That other car came over the line and sideswiped me," the motorist says. But on checking, the policeman learns, from the skid marks, that it was the other way around—it was the speaker's car that had gone over the center line. Yet, the motorist might have sincerely believed he was telling the truth!

Getting the truth is not always easy. It's not that people are dishonest. Other obstacles may intervene. Listen to what Dr. Edgar James Swift, a psychologist at Washington University has to say:

"My experiments have proved to me that, in general, when the average man reports events or conversations from memory and conscientiously believes that he is telling the truth, about one-fourth of his statements are incorrect, and this tendency to false memory is the greater the longer the time since the original experience."

This happens even when the observer has no personal axe to grind. How much harder it is to get a straight story when his emotions are involved!

Uses of the truth

To manage people, you need the truth. The logic of your reasoning, the soundness of your decisions, the effectiveness of your actions demand that you have a solid foundation in fact.

There are many occasions when your management of people requires that you know the truth. Without it, you're stymied. With it, you can use your judgment, your sense of fairness and exert your authority to the most desirable ends. For example, here are some of the situations in which getting the truth is of primary importance to your leadership:

. . . *errors.* A mistake has been made. To remedy it, you must have the truth. I remember one particularly dramatic instance, told to me by the plant manager of a solvents firm:

"We use inert nitrogen in one of our vapor systems, to minimize the danger of explosion. By mistake, an employee hooked in a container of volatile hydrogen. It was discovered, and then we had to know how much hydrogen there was in the system. That depended on how long the hydrogen had been feeding in. The man told me that it had been for about 20 minutes. We stopped everything, cleared all personnel out of buildings. Then, using long-handled wrenches, we opened the safety valves, and the danger was over. The employee had told the truth. If he hadn't, the outcome might have been disastrous."

The truth, in this instance, had saved lives and prevented a serious explosion.

. . . *friction.* A quarrel breaks out between two members of a service club. You step forward to quell it. "He used insulting language to me," says Member A. "He started it," insists B. "He called me a blankety-blank first." You've got to get to the bottom of the disagreement, to know the real honest-to-goodness basis for the argument, to be able to decide who's doing what to whom, and to settle the argument fairly.

. . . *lateness, absenteeism.* You're on a committee set up to plan for your church group. One of the five committee members is either late or absent on the nights meetings are called.

"Bob just isn't interested," one of the members says.

"I talked to him yesterday," says another. "He says Tuesday nights are bad for him. He has to work late at the office."

"Hogwash. It's just an excuse. We all have time problems. He's just afraid to come right out and tell us the truth . . ."

Before you know how to handle Bob's case, you've got to know what's really up.

You can add your own situations that cry out for the truth, before you can act. They'll range from problems of poor performance to morale to motivation. At every turn, it's the same story: you must get the truth before you can move.

Why do you want it, anyway?

Before we go any further, let's ask a rather disconcerting question: "Why do you want the truth?"

One answer seems obvious. You may say, "Mr. Uris, you explained that just a few moments ago. You said, 'The logic of one's reasoning, the soundness of one's decisions, the effectiveness of one's actions demand a solid foundation in fact.'"

Yes, that explains what we do with the truth in a functional sense. But the question being raised now has to do with your *purpose* in seeking the truth. For example:

A lawyer may want the truth to win his case. This may mean sending a man to the electric chair or sending him out to freedom. In either case, he's seeking a legal victory.

Secret police of a dictatorship may "want the truth"—and try to get it by torture. They may want it to destroy an anti-government faction, to kill off the opposition.

A social worker seeks the truth to discharge society's obligations fairly, to see that a person in real need is helped, one who is trying to pull a fast one, is pointed to the door.

In your overall plan to manage and master people, your purpose in probing for the truth is always constructive. Your motive is almost like the doctor's. He pursues the truth to be able to help his patient. You seek the truth to help the individual, to help your organization, to help make yourself a more effective leader. One purpose that certainly must not be yours is that of the snooper, the person whose probing is motivated by morbid curiosity. Once you've gotten enough facts to carry out your objective, you stop.

Setting the world to rights

In some ancient Greek dramas, and in some Shakespearean ones, the play ends in a very significant way. Take *Hamlet*, for instance. After the multiple tragedy of the last scene, when almost all the principals of the drama lie dead on the stage, what happens? Fortinbras appears, and restores order. It is the restoration of order, in a very practical sense, that is often your purpose in getting the truth. You seek the truth, for example, in order to settle a feud amicably. Here's a true story that has come to be a classic in the business world.

It's the case of a project manager in an electronics firm who suspected that someone was pilfering supplies. He didn't want to accuse or punish any individuals. In fact, he didn't even want to know who they were. He simply wanted to put a stop to the practice.

One day, he set a valuable micrometer down on his desk. He left the department for a few minutes. When he returned, the micrometer was gone.

He called the whole department over and said, "There's been a micrometer stolen. Now I don't care who took it. I just want to make sure it's returned, and that this kind of behavior stops. I'm going to turn off the lights, and I want the guilty party to put the micrometer on my desk."

The lights were turned off. One minute went by, two, then three. The lights went on, and there on the desk were *half a dozen* micrometers.

That manager had discovered more of the truth than he had expected. And in some cases, you may, too. But keep in mind that, as a responsible manager of people, it's up to you not to misuse what you learn or to probe past the point where you've learned all you need know to take constructive action to "restore order."

Obstacles to the truth

"Truth," said Kuan Ti, third century Chinese scholar, "is not like an ocean, open to all, but like a secret, guarded pool."

The Chinese philosopher's picture of the truth as something hidden and difficult to get at is accurate. Positive obstacles often stand in our way to the truth:

"Why should I level with you?" the tough kid tells his teacher. From his point of view, telling the truth is just sissy behavior. It's "square" to tell the truth, particularly to anyone in authority. In short, some people have no regard for the truth, and don't care whether they tell the truth or not.

"What's in it for me?" Some people go further than the recalcitrant youngster. They avoid telling the truth because of a lack of positive incentive. No payoff, no dice. "What will happen if I tell you?" asks the unwilling witness, brought into the police station for questioning. Fear of punishment is frequently an obstacle to getting the truth.

The seven truth-getting tools

Regardless of the obstacles put in your path, you must still be able to overcome them and get the facts you're after. Shortly, you will be given seven methods you can use to pierce through the opposition people may put up.

Keep in mind, however, that frequently the problem isn't to overcome people's resistance, but to help them assemble their thoughts or jog their memories.

When a witness in a court of law raises his hand and swears, "to tell the truth, the whole truth and nothing but the truth," he's undertaken a tall order. Getting the truth, in some cases, means you have to provide the help that makes it possible for a man or woman to get clear in his own mind exactly what the facts are.

Francis L. Wellman, one of the great masters of the art of legal cross-examination, has explained what the requirements are for getting the truth in a courtroom:

"It requires the greatest ingenuity; a habit of logical thought; clearness of perception in general; infinite patience and self-control; power to read men's minds intuitively, to judge of their characters by their faces, to appreciate their motives; ability to act with force and precision; a masterful knowledge of the subject matter itself; an extreme caution; and above all, the instinct to discover the weak point in the witness under examination."

As enlightening as Wellman's words are, don't forget he's talking specifically of the problem that besets the lawyer in the courtroom situation. Your quest for the truth usually takes place in less stringent surroundings. Furthermore, as you will soon see, the seven tools now to be described encompass most of Wellman's requirements, and do so in a clear, simple, easy to follow manner. Read 'em—and reap!

1. Tell them what's at stake

You may remember this key scene in the ancient Hollywood gangster movies. A call comes into the police station: "We've got to have someone who can open a bank vault. Can you locate an expert to do it?"

The police captain says no one on his staff has the ability. "But there's a man in town, now a respected citizen who used to be one of the country's outstanding safecrackers. Only trouble is, since he's gone straight, he's never admitted to being a safecracker."

Next scene shows the bank president, the nervous clerk and the distraught mother calling on the ex-felon. He steadfastly denies his real identity until the mother cries out, "My little boy is locked in that safe!"

The ex-felon then admits his identity and rushes off to practice his old trade. As we all remember, a little sandpaper on the fingertips and he succeeds in opening the safe and the child is restored to his parents.

For some people, in some situations, the fastest way to get the cold facts is to tell them what's involved. In the movie story, it was a child's life: It may be anything from a person's peace of mind to matters involving cash, a career or an individual's safety. But in all such situations, the same rule applies: bring home to the person who is reluctant to level with you exactly what's at stake. Be specific: "My little boy's life is at stake!" cries out the frightened parent. Or, the club leader says, "Tom, unless you tell us what happened between you and Fred, the group is going to divide into factions and that means the end of the club."

2. Provide an incentive

"What? Can money buy the truth?" you may ask.

In some instances, yes. Just remember some of the recent spy cases that made the headlines. Cash has made traitors of many. The favors of beautiful women are also used in espionage circles to get security facts.

Interestingly enough, by the same token, cash can create a lie. Christine Keeler, the notorious English party girl, was said to have offered a thousand pounds ($2,800) to a witness to give false testimony in an assault case involving Miss Keeler and an ex-boy friend.

But in the situations in which you find yourself searching for the truth, the incentives you provide needn't be cash or any other type of material benefit.

One executive tells an employee, "By helping us find out who is guilty of this senseless vandalism, you can make this a better place to work for everybody."

Not cash, but idealism, an appeal to a person's better self, is often the incentive that unlocks the hidden door to the truth.

3. Minimize the consequences

"If I tell," a frightened lad tells a youth leader, "the gang will beat my teeth in."

Sometimes an individual fears to tell the truth because he may be punished or he fears a painful kickback. You can certainly sympathize. Why should a man want to put his own head on the block? Nevertheless, when you come up against this situation, you have three courses open to you:

a. You can say, "You don't have to be afraid of any painful consequences. I will see to it that nothing will happen." Of course, it is a tack you take only when you can make good on your promise.

b. You may be able to point out that the consequences of *not* revealing the truth will be worse. "If you tell the truth, you're going to make Henry mad at you. But if you don't, the whole department will be down on you."

c. The situation may be one in which you can say: "Pete, you're exaggerating the consequences. Instead of thinking less of you, Madge will respect you all the more for taking the difficult but honest course."

4. Use the low-pressure approach

To some people, the essence of truth-getting seems to require shouting and bullying. In ordinary situations, the third-degree will get you no place. A more fruitful, and generally applicable approach is exactly the *opposite* of the get-tough manner.

Remember, in an earlier chapter, we discussed the use of silence as a means of getting people to reveal themselves? In getting the truth, the pause can be particularly effective. Don't feel you have to fill every second with talk. When you pause, you give the other person the urge to talk more.

Francis L. Wellman, in his book, *The Art of Cross-Examination*, says:

> Sometimes, it is useful not even to suggest the vital question until the witness has left the witness chair and has gone half-way to his seat. Then suddenly call him back, as if you had forgotten some detail—and quickly get the answer wanted amidst his excitement in having to resume his testimony.

However, you don't have to resort to any courtroom trickery. The low-pressure approach suggests that instead of trying to put pressure on an individual from the *outside,* you let him, in his doubts and uncertainties, build up internal pressures that will eventually force him to reveal what you want to know.

Skillful use of questions assist this process, and we'll be coming to the use of questions as a special tool in a short while. But, to conclude this point about use of the pause, the "soft" approach, here's the way one executive put it to work: "Mary, I know you well enough to be sure in my own mind that you would never distort the truth. Now let's go over the incidents in that meeting, and see if together we can't pin down exactly what happened. Now, remember when the meeting started . . ."

Stressing that he took it as a matter of course that the girl wanted to tell the truth proved to be the best possible approach.

5. Use facts to get more facts

In your quest for the facts, you usually hold a few minor ones in your hand. Used properly, you can build upon the facts you know to get the whole story. For example:

"O.K., Frankie," says the camp counselor, trying to get to the bottom of a near-riot among one of his groups, "we know that there were four boys in the clearing at the time, and you were one of them. Now start from the beginning . . ."

A variation of this approach is to use your partial knowledge to pick out weak points in someone's testimony. Just watch out that you don't set a trap for *yourself*.

One of the most famous legal proceedings of all time was the libel suit brought against the critic John Ruskin by the American artist, James McNeill Whistler.

Whistler especially complained of Ruskin's statement: "I have seen and heard much of Cockney impudence before now; but never expected to hear a coxcomb ask 200 guineas for flinging a pot of paint in the public's face."

The English Attorney General attempted to belittle Whistler's artistry:

"Can you tell me," asked the lawyer of the artist, "how long it took you to knock off that painting?"

"Two days," replied Whistler.

"The labor of two days then is that for which you ask 200 guineas?"

"No. I ask it for the knowledge of a lifetime!"

Incidentally, lawyers who are expert at cross-examination make it a practice to deadpan any telling points that are made to the detriment of their case. The best course for the Attorney General to have followed in the face of Whistler's devastating comeback would have been to shrug, say, "Just so, just so," and go on to the next point.

In your search for facts, your partial knowledge may not only help you develop more facts, but may put you in a position to spot an obvious untruth masquerading as its opposite. For example:

A supervisor in a canning plant was trying to get to the bottom of an error that resulted in the contamination of a vat of candied cherries. "Harry," he tells an employee from the maintenance crew, "you've been trying to tell me that you didn't do any painting in the Mixing Room yesterday. I know at least three people who saw you up on the scaffold over the vat 15 minutes before quitting time. Now why don't you level with me . . ."

Once you trip up a man, you're in a stronger position to urge him to drop all pretense and make a clean breast of it.

One variant, to be used with caution, is to pose the *opposite* of facts you already know. The individual may jump to clear up the mistake. For example, here's the way one executive got the lowdown on the cause of an error:

"As I understand it, you think Ralph failed to put through the order?" The answer came, "Oh, no, it wasn't Ralph . . ." And then the man had to admit his own responsibility.

And now we come to one of the most incisive tools that exists for getting the truth. It's an art in itself, yet part of every other approach. The tool in question is the question mark.

6. Learn how to use the question mark

The question mark by its very shape suggests a hook. Used properly, you can use it to hook the truth once and for all. But the use of questions is no haphazard machine gun affair. There are different types of questions and each has its specific use. Here's how to put the question mark to use:

a. *Start with a general question.* For one thing, it gets the session going smoothly. It also serves to ease the tension.

The very broad question can bring surprising results. That may happen if the individual has something on his mind, of which the questioner is not even aware.

You probably recall the old chestnut of the six-year old who asks, "Mom, where did I come from?" Mom collects her wits and launches into a full-scale discussion of the birds and bees. Billy listens patiently, then says, "But, Mom, where did I come from? A new kid down the block says he came from Cincinnati."

The chief clerk in a bank tells this incident. He'd been out ill when the monthly statements were processed and heard on his return that they had not gone out on time. Hoping to improve procedures he asked one of his key employees, "Ellen, what do you think we can do to speed up the monthly statements?"

Much to his surprise, the girl tearfully gushed out a tale of hitherto well-concealed but bitter conflict between herself and another book-keeper. It had erupted the night they were doing the statements, with a devastating effect on the work. Here the truth emerged abruptly, but helpfully, because of a general question.

b. *Avoid leading or loaded questions.* The leading question, a fa-vorite in cross-examining hostile witnesses, is banned by the courts on *direct examination* of a friendly witness. As a general rule, it should be left out of your repertoire for the same reason courts dislike it: it sug-gests the answer you want and discourages the individual from giving his own.

When you say to an employee, "Wouldn't you agree that this is a better way?" you invite a "yes," though that may be the last answer he wants to give.

Loading a question has the same effect. You phrase it so that you indicate your own feeling and encourage him to conceal his. It's the old, "Have you stopped beating your wife" gambit. He knows he's licked no matter what he says—so why try?

To ask a man, "How come you were so unforgivably careless?" is a way to close his mouth.

c. *Use "yes" or "no" questions sparingly.* To get much informa-tion, you would need a lot of them. Save them for the occasions when you want to pin down a single fact. For one thing, a flat yes or no often leaves you flat, especially if the answer is untrue.

More important, you can't get much idea of a person's feeling from a monosyllabic response. Since a big part of your truth-seeking function is to help the interviewee see the truth as it exists, full ex-pression of his thoughts and emotions is valuable.

d. *Avoid "machine gun" questions.* Certainly, law enforcement people and lawyers use it, but only when they are almost positive they have a liar on their hands. The rapid, staccato attack is intended to confuse and entrap, and could make a perjurer out of a saint. Your attitude must make it clear that you and he are engaged in a joint enterprise to uncover the truth.

Give him time to think, encourage him to take his time, concen-trate and so on. This is the very opposite of such pressure tactics as the stream of harsh questions, intended to trip him up.

e. *Prod with indirect questions.* These help you get an elaboration of what's been said before. For instance, you might keep this formula in mind: "Can you spell that out in more detail?" Or try, "I'm not quite sure I understand."

7. Build truthfulness by building confidence

One way to thaw hostility and resistance is to build a feeling of confidence toward you in the other person.

For example, it's been said of the famous trial lawyer, Rufus Choate, that he never aroused opposition on the part of a witness by attacking him. Choate's course was to disarm him by a quiet and courteous manner, a show of simple friendliness.

Professor Mary K. Keeley of New York University, with wide experience in handling parole, delinquency and related interview situations, has pointed out:

"Don't expect people to trust you right away. Suspicion, hostility, doubt, anxiety, are all normal and to be predicted. The individual is wary not only about what the person asking questions will think of him, but also wary about how the material will be used." And she adds, "You can do almost anything in an interview situation if you can convince the person you are doing it for his own benefit."

Francis L. Wellman points out the two sides of the coin in the courtroom:

> If the cross-examiner allows the witness to suspect that he distrusts his integrity, he will straighten himself in the witness chair and mentally defy him at once. If, on the other hand, the counsel's manner is courteous and conciliatory, the witness will soon lose his fear and can be induced to enter into a discussion in a fair-minded spirit.

Sometimes, the problem isn't to get the truth, but to *recognize it*.

Understand what they say from their point of view

An executive on his way to the parking lot sees a group of employees boarding a bus. He spots one girl in the group trying to push aboard with a tray of expensive parts in her hand.

Excitedly, he pulls the girl back and demands an explanation.

"Mr. Smith told me this is what I should do," she replies.

"That's absurd. Come back to the plant and we'll see about this."

Back to the plant they go. "Smith," he says to the girl's foreman, "she says you told her to . . ."

"Marge, how could you say such a thing? You know that's not true."

"Why it is, Mr. Smith. You told me to put these parts on the bus at the end of the day."

"On the bus? Oh, for crying out loud."

To the new girl, the "bus" was the vehicle that took her home rather than the cart used in the plant for moving parts from one area to another!

In pinning down the truth, be sure you really understand what's been said. Don't be thrown off the track by words, phrases, whole statements, whose import you're not clear on. Your protection is the question mark. Keep asking questions until you're completely sure of what's been said.

Don't stand in your own way

One of the most serious obstacles to the truth is often the leader who stands in his own way.

Dr. George Goldman, associate clinical professor of psychiatry of the Columbia Psychoanalytical Clinic says, "The interviewer must be aware of his own attitudes and their impact on the other person before he can even begin to assess the individual."

That means you may be your own problem. Here are some of the things you have to watch in yourself.

. . . *your emotions.* Usually you have a stake in the outcome of your quest. The mere fact that you have to search for the truth is likely to cause you some annoyance. You may be angry, fearful or frustrated. At least during the time you're digging for the truth you have to put a firm brake on your feelings.

. . . *your biases.* Everybody has them. In the instance of truth-finding they warp your judgment. For instance, you may have a grudge against the person you're questioning. You're more likely to think ill of him, be overly suspicious, be quick to show your hostility. Again, you have to curb these feelings to increase the chances of your getting the truth.

. . . *your preconceptions*. Ideally you should have none. But as a practical matter you must have at least a tentative theory to start your investigation. It's important for you to be ready to discard your belief when information you get suggests a weak foundation.

. . . *your haste to judge*. "Reserve decision" is a phrase often heard in the courtroom. It means that the judge wants time to think things over.

Expert analysts make it a practice to note *but not pass judgment* on each fact presented. Later they weigh all the evidence before coming to a decision.

Overcome the natural tendency to form an opinion on each point as you hear it. Wait until you have heard everything before drawing a firm conclusion.

Finally, you have to face up to a tough situation, unpleasant, but unavoidable:

When the "truth" is a lie

In any approach to getting the truth, you must face up to an ultimate possibility: What do you do when you're told "the truth" and it's obvious that it's a lie. When this situation occurs it's serious. How should you handle it?

The experts agree here on only one thing: You *don't* ignore it. That's harmful to both you and the would-be deceiver. If the latter is a child, this may be the bad experience that makes it difficult for him to tell the truth. If it's an adult you may be reinforcing his secret belief that he can "get away with anything."

In such cases, there are three basic ways you have of meeting the lie:

. . . express your disbelief plainly.

. . . confront the individual with the objective evidence that contradicts him.

. . . keep him talking until he trips himself.

And finally, give him the chance of straightening himself out. Make one sharp and final request for the truth. This situation is certainly one where reasonable punishment must be meted out on continued failure to level with you.

▶ RECAP ◀

In this chapter we've covered one of the toughest, most demanding, and at the same time, one of the most rewarding areas of dealing with people. The subject of getting the truth comes in in dozens of situations, on the job and off. Here are the major points we covered:

The tool: how to get the truth.

When to use it: when you need to know the facts, in order to help an individual, your organization, to advance a worthwhile activity or to make yourself a more effective leader.

How to develop it: these are the key techniques you use to sharpen your truth-getting capabilities:

1. Tell them what's at stake.
2. Provide an incentive.
3. Minimize the consequences.
4. Use the low-pressure approach.
5. Use facts to get more facts.
6. Learn to use the question mark.
7. Build truthfulness by building confidence.

Finally, let these principles guide your use of the seven truth-getting tools:

. . . understand what they say from *their* viewpoint.

. . . don't stand in your own way.

. . . know what to do when the truth is a lie.

chapter 8

To manage people, you have
to know how to talk to them.
For the most part, your face-to-
face relations with individuals
may represent only minor problems. Ordinary subject matter,
routine exchanges, can be
taken in stride.

But one of the marks of
the effective manager of people is his ability to talk to
people about subjects that are
the *very opposite* of routine.
They may be delicate, they
may be explosive. They may
touch on the deep, innermost
feelings of one or more people.
They may be intensely personal or they may be of a
highly confidential nature.

In any and all of these
cases, you have to proceed
with sureness and certainty,
realizing to the fullest extent
the hazards and pitfalls that
surround you, yet confident in
your own ability to handle the
situation. You must cover these
touchy subjects, retaining control, at the same time helping
the other person keep his own
balance.

how to
talk about
touchy subjects

It is this ability of the leader to walk sure-footedly, where fools rush in, and angels fear to tread, that sets him in a position of superiority. This one tool, almost always ably wielded by the highly experienced and mature leader, can give you an outstanding advantage in mastering people.

Perhaps this is a capability you may think you never could possess. It may seem to require an intellect of exceptional order, or to require the professional background of a doctor, lawyer, or clergyman.

Yet, with such professional training, perhaps the skill might already be yours. But now it lies mere minutes in your future. In the pages ahead you will find directions so clear and explicit, that acting on them will be child's play. And remember: these procedures have been pre-tested, have been refined and developed by the thousands of managers of people with whom I have worked over the years.

I came in out of the snow one cold January morning, to call on the president of a large printing firm in Queens. Five, ten minutes past the appointment time, twenty minutes, and the executive still had failed to have me summoned from the reception room. I was about to suggest that the receptionist find out the reason for the delay, when the president came out, shook hands quickly and ushered me into his office.

It was obvious that he was under tension. His face was flushed and moist, and his conversation was rapid and almost incoherent. In his office, he flopped into his chair and drew a deep breath.

"You'll have to excuse me, Mr. Uris, but I've just been through an ordeal," he said. Then he went on to explain that he had just fired one of his maintenance men, a man he had originally hired out of the goodness of his heart because a friend of the worker's had told a story of great need.

"And after all I did for him, he made himself a miserable job record here. His attendance was poor, he gave his foreman constant trouble. And can you imagine, after all this he had the nerve to give me an argument. What ingratitude!"

What makes a touchy subject?

As I sat listening to the top executive's tale, I couldn't help but wonder more at the man who was telling it than about the story itself. After all, this was the top man in a very large enterprise. Granted, that firing an employee is never pleasant, but why was he so worked up over the matter?

I then recalled a questionnaire I had seen a few weeks previous, that had been sent to sales executives across the country. One question had been: "What do you consider the toughest part of your job?"

The answer of a large percentage had been, "Firing an employee."

Here in the printing company president's office was direct evidence of the difficulty. But why? I asked myself. What is it that makes certain subject areas so difficult for people?

To answer that question, we must dig below the surface. When we do, we find that there are three basic aspects to the problem.

1. What subjects are touchy?

2. What factors make them touchy?

3. How do you talk about these subjects "you'd rather not talk about"—and do so effectively?

The touchy subject

Sex is a touchy subject. We know that from all the jokes about the difficulty parents have in acquainting their offspring with the facts about the birds and bees.

We know there are certain subjects that are not fit for "mixed company." Certain biological facts of life are considered poor choices for subject matter in ordinary circles.

Religion, particularly in personal terms, is another subject that you often have been told is a good one—to avoid.

A man's personal relationships—with his parents, his wife, even his children, often fit into the conversational never-never land.

Getting into job areas, we've seen that firing of employees tends to be out of bounds.

A person's physical disfigurement or handicap is generally skirted like a conversational quicksand. One unsuccessful attempt to avoid such a subject met with disaster that time has not erased.

The story is told of a charming female member of the Astor family who was to entertain the great J. P. Morgan at tea. Aside from great wealth and power, Morgan's oversized nose was his outstanding characteristic. He was very sensitive about it. Mrs. Astor told her young teenage daughter to avoid absolutely any mention of Mr. Morgan's visage. "As a matter of fact," said Mrs. Astor, "don't for heaven's sake even use the word *nose* in a sentence."

The afternoon progressed smoothly. Mr. Morgan was an able conversationalist, and Mrs. Astor, with a sigh of relief, saw the end of her trial in view.

Finally in came the tea things. Mrs. Astor poured. Mr. Morgan accepted his cup of tea, and his hostess asked sweetly, "Mr. Morgan, would you like some sugar in your nose?"

Sometimes, our very attempts to stay out of trouble precipitate it.

All the subjects mentioned above are difficult to handle in a conversation. Ordinarily, you might choose to avoid them, and probably wisely so.

But in managing people, you often find you must enter these inflammable subject areas in order to accomplish some desirable objective. For example, you may have to talk to a handicapped person about his infirmity, so that you can help him cope with a work problem. You may have to talk to a female employee about her home situation, to be able to help her improve a poor attendance problem.

The factors that cause the trouble

Before going into the specific guidelines that provide you with the know-how you need to move successfully in this critical area, let's probe more deeply into the question: What makes a touchy subject touchy? With this analysis accomplished, you'll find you can handle the problem with greater understanding and confidence.

Let's take some typical examples, put them under the X-ray, and see what it is that causes the trouble:

The case of the stuttering suitor

This was told to me by Don R, a personal friend, now many years happily married. Don said, "I met my wife at college, the University of Pennsylvania, where we were both students. We had a brief but wonderful courtship and decided to get married right after graduation.

"The problem was that she came from an old Baltimore family, and I was from the wrong side of the tracks. My father was a small restaurant owner in Brooklyn, and as far as Helen's family was concerned, that was the bottom of the social ladder.

"I'll never forget the ordeal I went through when I had to ask her parents for their consent to our marriage. Oh, I don't mean to say that if they had said no, there'd have been no marriage. It was more or less a formality. But I was so upset, that even though I knew Helen's parents fairly well, I stuttered through the entire conversation. Getting out each word took an effort. It was one of the most miserable experiences of my life."

Perhaps you'd like to analyze this situation, decide for yourself why my friend suffered so badly, and then compare notes with me. If you want to stop reading right here, take a minute off and think about the story.

As I see it, there were two basic factors that made the request for Helen's hand a touchy subject:

A. *The stakes were high.* After all, Don's entire future depended on the outcome of this meeting. Marriage is one of the most critical actions a person ever takes in his life, and Don was very much aware that in the course of his conversation he was carving out the future pattern of his life. An unsettling thought? Of course. Any subject you talk about on which great decisions or great changes depend is bound to be touchy.

Then, there was another factor in this case that added to Don's difficulty:

B. *He felt at a disadvantage.* It's one thing to conduct a conversation with an equal, a person with whom you feel at ease. But Don had made it abundantly clear that he considered himself socially inferior to his fiancée's family. And because he felt inferior, felt exposed and in a sense defenseless, a conversation that might have been cordial and friendly was strained and painful.

You too will find that if either party to a conversation feels at a disadvantage, the subject matter somehow becomes explosive. Raw nerves are exposed, innocent phrases take on deep emotional color, and any emotional content becomes plain dynamite.

The case of the upset boss

Let's return to the Queens printing company president for our second example.

We know that firing people is never pleasant or easy to do. But in the situation described earlier in this chapter, it is clear that the executive's reaction was extreme. Why?

Again, if you'd care to test your own powers of analysis, take a minute or two now, and either recall or reread the description. Then decide why the top executive was upset.

Here's my analysis:

A. *There was a failure involved.* As you may remember, the executive "out of the goodness of his heart," as he saw it, had given the man a job and his gesture had kicked back. The man's failure to perform meant that the president's efforts, too, had failed.

You'll find whenever you have to talk to someone about a poor performance or a failure of greater or lesser degree, the heat is on. And when you yourself are involved in the failure, the atmosphere is likely to get close, and the tension is likely to build.

B. *Ego feelings were involved.* The company president was reacting to the situation because his ego was being manhandled.

Remember, in Chapter 3 we talked about the self-image? Well, the executive, by his generous act, felt himself to be a kind-hearted, philanthropic person. Now, the man's failure to show his appreciation, and further, the show of ingratitude, shattered the executive's favorable self-image.

The employee forced the executive into a position he found unpleasant and undesirable, namely, that of a "harsh employer." This change, from self-approval to a certain amount of guilt, was pretty rough on the executive's feelings about himself. The degree of emotional upset has already been described.

Now, one more example:

The case of the rose who didn't smell like one

The division head of a West Coast metal products company tells this story:

"We had a girl on the inspection staff who suffered from body odor. Naturally, it was embarrassing and a problem to everyone. The question was how could this situation be brought to the attention of the young lady without doing serious injury to her feelings? Even her supervisor balked at the thought."

What were the factors deterring the supervisor? Test your own powers of analysis either mentally or in writing and note what there was about this problem that made it difficult to discuss.

Here's my analysis:

A. *Personal pride.* Any time you have to tell a person something that either directly or indirectly hurts his self-esteem you've got an explosive subject. In Rose's case, acquainting her with an unpleasant fact about herself, and still further by so doing having her understand that some and perhaps all of her co-workers were aware of her personal problem, would certainly hurt.

B. *Status in the group.* The second damaging point involved for Rose was the fact that she would see her status in the group undermined and wrecked.

These three instances dramatize the problem that you face. They not only illustrate actual instances of touchy conversational areas, but also provide insights into the basic elements that are causing the trouble.

Eight rules that arm you against trouble

By a careful analysis of many cases similar to the three you've just read, a set of principles have been evolved that make it possible for you to tread on dangerous ground and not only come off unscathed but achieve constructive and worthwhile objectives.

As you read the following rules, apply them mentally to situations that you know about firsthand, that you may have witnessed among your friends, family or people with whom you work:

1. *Ask yourself, "Is there something to be gained by discussing the matter?"*

Too often the novice feels that all problems must be attacked at once and in force. But study the way an experienced and successful manager of people operates. You'll notice that in many cases he permits an undesirable situation to exist for days, weeks, even months. Why?

In many cases it's because he has the feeling that the time is not ripe for him to open up the question. However, another possibility, and this is one never to be discounted, is that he has made a decision that may be worded this way: "It's better to live with this problem and put up with the inconvenience it causes than to risk the consequences of attempting to eliminate it."

Cowardly? Unwise? Probably neither. The fact is you occasionally do find situations which are better ignored. For example:

Lon Heuser, foreman in a Massachusetts building materials supply company told me: "One day I happened to turn a corner too fast down at the shop and came across three of my most trusted men pitching quarters. There was a clear-cut company policy that gambling was forbidden on company premises. I suppose I could have made a federal case of it. Instead I walked by as though I hadn't noticed anything. But the men got the idea well enough. They knew I knew and had decided not to do anything about it. But they also knew it was the kind of violation of regulations I would permit only once. I never had any further trouble with them."

If the problem you're concerned about is in the "touchy" area, be sure not to neglect the preliminary consideration: Should you attempt to deal with the problem at all? Your answer will be based on your knowledge of the seriousness of the situation and what you feel you have to gain or lose as a result of taking action.

2. *Should YOU be the one to do the talking?*

In many cases this is a responsibility you would not want to shirk. But occasionally a situation comes along in which a person other than yourself could do a much more effective job. Take the case of Rose, the inspector, with the problem of body odor. It's a common enough problem, as almost any personnel director will tell you. In almost all cases, they will agree with this advice:

The best possible person to talk to Rose would be not her supervisor but one of her co-workers, preferably an older, motherly-type woman who could tell her the score in a kindly and mature way. If you've picked the right person, Rose will end up with the feeling that no one else is on to her secret. And with the benefit of today's perfected deodorants, a major problem can quickly and easily be solved.

This same principle, by the way, should have been applied by the printing company president. It was neither his place nor responsibility to have laid off the troublesome maintenance man. The job should have been done either by the man's supervisor or someone from the personnel staff.

3. *Set the stage.*

Once you decide to act, be sure that you're stacking the cards as much as possible in your favor. Select a time and place that will make it possible to discuss the touchy subject with the maximum amount of privacy.

You do this for two reasons: First, because the chances are, in such surroundings, tensions will be most relaxed. Secondly, it's a way of telling the other person that you consider the matter important enough to deserve your full and undivided attention.

The "best place" for your conversation may be your living room, your private office or a friendly beer parlor. But whatever the time and place you've chosen, remember to try to suit the convenience of the other person. You don't want to add to his possible adverse reaction by putting him in a situation where he can say, "Do you mean to say you got me off in this out-of-the-way place just to talk about *that?*"

4. *Sound a favorable opening note.*

In all likelihood the person you're talking to will be somewhat apprehensive. You can usually calm such fears by starting off with a quiet sentence or two, for example: "Jim, there's a personal matter I've been wanting to talk to you about for some time. I thought it would be a good idea if we could get off together by ourselves so we won't be interrupted."

Exactly what your opening is depends on your relationship with the other person. If you know him well, a few minutes spent on general small talk may help to ease things.

However, *don't* make the mistake of a protracted opening. If you spend half an hour talking about the time you and Tom used to go fishing when you were kids and then suddenly veer around to letting him know that he's going to have to stop his torrid romance with one of the secretaries in the company, Tom would have every reason for surprise and resentment. The opening should be just that—a brief interlude intended to put the other person at ease and in a responsive frame of mind. Once you've done this, you're ready for the next step.

5. *Discuss the point at issue in a neutral, non-accusatory fashion.*

The problem here is to prevent the person you're talking to from becoming either defensive or hostile at the very outset. Notice the difference between these two approaches:

"I want to talk to you about your poor performance on the job."

"Tom, I'd like to talk to you about your job performance."

The first example is clearly going to arouse an undesirable reaction. The second, while it may put him somewhat on guard, still is going to make it possible for you to continue without having precipitated an argument or sour reaction.

6. *Give him a chance to state his case.*

"Helen," says her mother, "I told you you could have your friends in for the afternoon if you kept the house in order. Do you feel you've kept the bargain?"

Now Helen has the opportunity to tell her story. It may be anything from, "Why, Mom, what's wrong with the place?" to, "Looks all right to me," to, "Gee, I'm sorry, Mom, but the kids became absolutely unmanageable."

Notice that at this point you may either get accord or an argument but at least it's on a fairly calm and matter-of-fact basis.

7. *Help him save face.*

Failure to follow this single principle has probably caused more trouble, more upset and more failure than anything else. From child-rearing to international politics, the rule applies.

A skillful parent knows that he must give his child a chance to come off in a situation without looking too bad. Accordingly, his father tells Johnny, "This is the worst report card you've had in the last two years. Now I know these last three months have been hectic for you. You've been helping around the house, you've been staying down at school afternoons for baseball practice, and even doing odd jobs on weekends. Nevertheless . . ."

This wise parent, having given Johnny an out, can now go on to make the comments that can help get Johnny back on the track.

Diplomats use exactly the same tactics in international dealings. All you have to do to verify this point is to turn back to the newspaper files on the blockade of Cuba, imposed by President Kennedy in October of 1962. He drew a hard, fast line beyond which he wouldn't let the Russians go. And yet, despite the toughness of the blockade, he made it clear to Chairman Khrushchev that Russian *warships* would *not* be stopped on the high seas. This tacit admission of the inviolability of Russia's armed might was a face-saving device Khrushchev needed to be able to explain to his high command why he was going to accede to Kennedy's demands.

You help a man save face in a number of ways:

. . . accept his explanation of a situation: "I'm willing to go along with you, Henry, when you say you lost your head when you slapped Louise."

. . . minimize the most painful aspects of the situation. Take an instance in which a man's failure is the subject at hand. You might say, "True enough, Alf, your sales for the last quarter have been the lowest you've ever made. On the other hand, let's remember that generally you've been above average . . ."

. . . remind him of an "area of honor." Remember in the case of the "Stuttering Suitor" one of his problems was that he felt at a disadvantage. When you're dealing with a person who is in this situation, you can help him out by reminding him of areas of successful or worthwhile accomplishment. Don R., the Stuttering Suitor, should have *reminded himself* of some facts along these lines:

"I guess that as far as Helen's parents are concerned, I'm from the wrong side of the tracks. On the other hand, this means that I had a pretty tough struggle getting to where I am today. That makes me a pretty superior guy."

Similarly, you can remind a man that you may have to fire, "Let's face it squarely. You haven't made a go of this job. But I want you to know it's my personal opinion, that this doesn't at all reflect on your capabilities. I think you have the potential to be an outstanding technician. This job just wasn't suited to your particular skills. I repeat, you've got a lot on the ball . . ."

8. *Close on a positive note.*

The worst thing some people do is to let a talk on a touchy subject dribble off in a dreary, unconstructive, perhaps even inconclusive manner.

Avoid this at all costs. The feeling at the end of your talk is probably the one the man will take away with him. Therefore, plan for it as thoughtfully as you would any other phase. For example, here's the way one employer was able to end an interview with a man he had to demote:

"Cass, I don't want to kid you. This new job you're going to be in carries less responsibility and less pay than your previous one. On the other hand, don't forget these facts. First, if I didn't value your abilities I wouldn't be giving you another job. Second, I think this new situation is one that you can use to such good advantage that frankly I'll be surprised if, within a year's time, you're not even further ahead than you were in your previous position. Finally, let me assure you again of my personal friendship. I hope we'll be getting together from time to time for lunch or at some other occasion where we can talk things over and see how you're doing."

This executive is setting an excellent example to emulate. Notice particularly the closing note, the avowal of friendship and the intention to keep in touch. In many cases, this one point, reminding the other person of your warm feelings and friendly intentions can take the sting out of the most drastic correction or penalty.

The other points are also extremely effective. Note, for example, the emphasis on the regard for the man's capability and the encouragement for his future.

Eight pillars of wisdom

In these eight steps, taken together, you have a forge-hardened tool that can help you form a situation to your will. You can take the heat out of a controversy, remove the fuse from the most explosive issue.

Remember that to a large extent, your *manner* is an important part of the combination. If you speak without resentment, without accusation and castigation, you greatly reduce the likelihood of major resentment or blowup. By keeping the focus on the point at issue, the specific act or behavior, you keep the conversation direct and uncomplicated.

Analysis of many instances where terrific rows have broken out shows that core of the trouble has been that the person conducting the interview failed to control a conversation. Talk jumped from one point of sensitivity to another. This built up an emotional storm in the other person that eventually burst its bonds.

It is this type of mishandling that degenerates into yelling matches in which all logic disappears. That's when you hear the typical "Yes you are—no I'm not" type of dispute. You avoid this and other hazards by the eight steps that have been enumerated.

My recommendation is this: If at any time you find yourself facing a touchy situation, review the eight points. Think through—and you may want to write out, even partially memorize—the specifics you will use under each point. With this planning carefully done, with dec consideration given to the exact situation and the personality of the individual involved, you can't miss.

▶ RECAP ◀

Boiled down to essentials, here are the important points of this chapter:

The tool we've been talking about: How to talk about touchy subjects.

How and when to use it: You apply the tool when it becomes clear that you have to talk to an individual about a subject to which he is sensitive and is likely to react adversely.

How to develop the tool: You improve your ability to cover the "touchy subject" by using first your insight of the kind of factors that make subjects "touchy" in the first place:

—the stakes are high;

—the person feels at a disadvantage;

—there is a failure involved;

—ego feelings are laid on the line.

Finally you apply the eight "pillars of wisdom," the eight steps that can help you pick your way safely through the most sensitive areas:

1. Ask yourself, "Is there something to be gained by discussing the matter?"

2. Should YOU be the one to do the talking?

3. Set the stage.

4. Sound a favorable opening note.

5. Mention the point at issue in a neutral, non-accusatory fashion.

6. Give him a chance to state his case.

7. Help him save face.

8. Close on a positive note.

chapter 9

"The power to command is the power to achieve," said Lord Nelson.

In today's world, the great British hero's words take on special importance. Again and again we're told that the man who accomplishes great things in business, in his community, or in a professional field must know how to work through others. It's true, absolutely true. And yet, despite the importance of having others carry out our instructions, we witness one miserable failure after another. For example:

". . . and don't forget to see that the valve is open before you leave," instructs the manager.

"Sure thing, boss," the employee says. Next day, the distillery is in an uproar. Five thousand gallons of expensive alcohol have been run out of a storage tank and down the drain.

The manager had *meant* for the employee to open a valve in the heating system. The employee, who had been

**instructions
— how to
give orders
that get
results**

working around the storage tanks, naturally associated the valve in question with the one on the huge tank. And he carried out what he thought were his superior's commands—with serious loss to all.

Why orders go wrong

"Can't happen," you may say, "nobody is that stupid." But the fact is the errors, accidents and dollar losses due to fouled-up instructions are astronomical.

And the kickbacks from poorly delivered commands are measured in human as well as material terms:

"I'm not taking orders from that bossy so and so," explodes a member of a fraternal organization in Roosevelt, Long Island. The president had given him what was intended as a suggestion. But to the businessman, who had taken on the job of doing the publicity, he was being "ordered" around—and he resented it bitterly.

Of all the things you do in the mastery of people, the payoff point is usually the order or instructions you give. Yet for many, the payoff never takes place because they fumble at the critical point.

Proof? Just call to mind from your own experience a single instance of the failures that abound. Or, take as an example this instance of bubble-headed order-giving:

"Er, Frank, take that thingamajig over there. Well, it's not over there but you'll find it. And when you do, if it fits, place it over the opening of part #16—or maybe it's #17. . . ." etc. etc.

We all pity poor Frank, at the mercy of a soup-brained boss who will not only fail to get the action he wants, but will end up with an angry and frustrated assistant on his hands.

The kickbacks of poor order-giving resound in angry protest:

"That isn't what you said."

"I didn't think you meant you wanted it done *that* way."

"Did you mean . . ."

Order-giving at its best is lucid and precise. You get the performance you want from people by giving orders that they can carry out promptly and accurately because they understand *two* things:

. . . what you've said.

. . . what you meant.

By composing your orders according to a simple set of principles, you make them trouble-free. At the same time you won't be putting your people in a strait jacket. You give them the opportunity to use their initiative and imagination, at the same time you get the results *you* want.

The sure road to order-giving results

The beautiful thing about order-giving is that there's a minimum of mystery to an effective approach. By now, both the theory and practice of instruction have been highly developed on the business scene. The amazing thing is that despite this sure-fire knowledge, despite the years of dependable experience, executives of even the highest echelons sometimes develop a bad case of foot-in-mouth disease in giving instructions.

Why?

The answer seems to be that they have failed to systematize their order-giving technique. They flout the rules, and hope to get results anyhow. Are they wrong? You bet they are. While the method they use may work nine times out of ten, that tenth time results in a fiasco simply because their instructions have omitted a key element. And they'll be more amazed than anyone at their oversight.

Seven steps to effectiveness

When you master the seven principles given below, you will find yourself on a par with the most successful order-givers in the business. Of course, for ordinary requests, you needn't check through the principles. If all you want is simple acquiescence to, "Mary, please hand me the Smith file," you can proceed almost automatically.

But when the orders are important or if your experience in giving instructions has been limited, applying seven simple rules will guarantee you top action. Here, now, are the seven steps you need keep in mind to maximize the results people turn in when you issue your instructions:

Rule No. 1—Be sure you know the result you want

The chairwoman of an organization formed to raise funds for the expansion of a Miami hospital recently worked herself into a chaotic situation. A dinner-dance was to be given in a local hall. Materials for decorating had been delivered and with great zeal the chairlady and ten eager assistants proceeded to get the hall ready for the event.

"Mary and Helen, you put the crepe streamers across the two beams. Sharon, you and Hester start arranging the flowers across that wall over there. Now the rest of us will start setting the tables."

After a half hour a shriek of dismay arose from one of the working crews. "We can't put the streamers up on those beams. That's where the lights will be coming from." And the ladies who had been distributing the flowers similarly had to undo their work because the wall that had been designated was the one where the orchestra would have to stand.

Yes, you have to know the state of affairs you want to bring about before you can tell anyone to do anything. There's a fine distinction to be made here. It isn't always necessary for you to know *how* the job is to be done. For example, you can give the instruction: "Keep adding color until the paint in both drums is identical." If that order is given to a trained color-matcher, then the exact method he uses to get his result is *his* business.

At the same time, it's essential that you *never* give orders that require action beyond the ability of the person you're instructing. I recall an embarrassing failure of my own along these lines. In my supervisory days, I'd hired a young man as an inspector and since we were rushed, put him to work almost immediately:

"Mike, measure these discs," I told him, "and set aside all those that measure more than .500."

When I came back half an hour later not a disc had been inspected and the young man was standing, red-faced, fiddling around with the micrometer.

"What's wrong?" I asked.

"I'm sorry but I don't know how to use this type of micrometer."

In special cases you may have to insert a checkback in your instructions. This is true when you're uncertain of how a part of your instructions will turn out. Accordingly, you may say, "When you get to that stage, let me know and then we'll decide what the next step should be."

Rule No. 2—Prepare the order either in your mind or in writing

When orders involve critical matters or complicated business, you want to make sure that you're overlooking no bets. Your best insurance is to spell them out either mentally or in writing.

One of the best managers I ever knew was Fred Miller of the Tri-Plastic Moulding Corp. of Newark, New Jersey. Whenever he had to give orders involving more than one person, he'd map out the operation on a little chart like the one below.

	Phase 1, Hank	Phase 2, Pete	Phase 3, Jerry
When			
Where			
How			

This chart has several advantages. First, it puts the information down in black and white for each man to follow. Secondly, it lets each man know who else is on the job. And thirdly, each man can tell what the other fellow is responsible for, so that if they have to mesh procedures, they can figure out the means of doing it.

Rule No. 3—Select the right man for the job

In many cases the successful outcome of your order depends entirely on the person you select to carry it out. Certain orders, in fact, cannot be given at all, even though their objective is extremely important, because the right person to do the job is not available.

Consider the historical incident of the message to Garcia. It was only when the officers of the U.S. Military Intelligence were able to find a man qualified for the task—Lt. Andrew Somers Rowan—that contact with Gen. Calixto Garcia could be made.

In the average case you can make your selection on one simple point: who is available to act on the order? That is satisfactory when no unusual skills are required. But sometimes the problem is less simple, and in such cases you have to consider:

- Who is most available?
- Who is capable of the best performance?
- Who is in line to do the job?
- Who will best understand what is to be done?
- Who will be most cooperative or have the greatest drive to carry out the order?

There may be positive one-word answers to all these questions, and when there are you are in the clear. But frequently even these simple questions pose tough problems.

It is possible, for example, that the person most available to carry out your instructions may not be the person in line to do so.

Let's say you want a record made up of all the business contacts with a customer company. The assistant on whom you have depended for this type of assignment is tied up elsewhere. Another man capable of doing the job is available. Should you assign the second man?

Of course it depends in part on whether there is time pressure on the assignment, how long the "regular" man will be tied up, whether the substitute can really do the job to the standard that you require.

But before you decide, you've got to think over questions like these: Does the man on whom you usually depend for this kind of assignment think of it as "his" job? Will you set up an antagonism between the two subordinates by pulling a switch on previous practices?

You'll find your choice will depend largely on the emphasis the situation gives to the list of questions above. If, for example, the question of the quality of performance is paramount, you may cast all considerations aside, make sure that your best man gets the assignment.

Rule No. 4—Tailor-make your instructions for the person

"Which way to Catalina Island?" shouted the man at the wheel of a 30-foot power boat as it loomed alongside a weatherbeaten old cruiser. The captain got out his chart and parallel rules, calculating the course, then—

"Nor' nor'east by east," he shouted.

"Don't get technical," came the response, "just point."

A lot of people are like that. They get it better if you show them.

Sometimes you'll want to back up your oral instructions with charts, diagrams, illustrations or other visual material.

An important point here is to remember to pitch the instructions to the level of the person's understanding.

"Don't get technical, just point" is the kind of retort you can expect from a non-technical person. But you're just as likely to get the opposite kind of kickback: "I'm sorry, Sir, I don't understand your generalities," a lab technician said to his staff executive. "If you can tell me exactly what information you want . . ."

The experience, education, intelligence and verbal skills of the person you've selected for your order-giving key you in to the best style your order must follow to get the results you want. In general, be short and simple, but when the nature of the task is complicated you may have to spell out your instructions in full detail.

Rule No. 5—Suit the order to the situation

Dr. Robert N. Wilson in the magazine *Human Organization* describes the order-giving process in the amphitheater of the typical operating room:

"The individuals composing a (surgical) operating team are so close-knit and understand their techniques so thoroughly that verbal signals are often unnecessary."

And at the other end of the scale are the instructions developed for the vast military maneuver of the Normandy invasion, World War II. The written documents for this move would fill a room of over 200 cubic foot capacity.

Situations have a way of dictating an order-giving style. For example, the *Daily News* of September 4, 1963, reported a small blaze that broke out in a loft building on Spring Street in New York City. The owner of the enterprise issued the appropriate order with classic correctness:

"Fire! Everybody out!"

For the other side of the coin, watch some of Broadway's topnotch directors at work. They'll spend hours developing a characterization in order to get across to an actor the subtle and complex instructions they want followed.

Rule No. 6—Check for understanding

General Grant is said to have retained an incompetent officer on his staff for a single purpose. "If he can understand my orders, anyone can," explained Grant. You may not be able to keep such weather vanes to test the intelligibility of your orders, but you have other means available.

Any doubt you have about whether you have been understood can be resolved by methods like these:

(a) Get your subordinate to repeat your instructions.

(b) If you feel course (a) may offend him, you may check indirectly by asking: "How do you plan to go about it?"

One thing to watch at this point. Don't use the traditional "Got it?" with an individual you don't know too well.

Experienced order-givers will tell you that a person who hasn't gotten it will often say O.K. not because he understands what you want, but because he doesn't want to seem stupid.

The "got it" approach is usually adequate when the man you're working with is a known quality. When you're in doubt, your check should be aimed at making sure he really understands. Some managers make a check by asking questions:

"Do you understand why the customer's code number should be placed in the upper left corner of Form A?"

"Do you understand why the temperature can't drop below a hundred?"

Your final guarantee of 100% results lies in:

Rule No. 7—Check for progress

It's happened time and time again.

If you listen carefully you may even be able to hear the words echoing either in reality or through your memory:

"But I told you . . ."

"How could you have misunderstood . . .?"

The fact is that despite the best-intentioned and conscientious performance of the first six steps of effective order-giving, failure to include No. 7 may lead to trouble.

There are several ways to check your order-giving:

a. *Make periodic inspections.* For certain kinds of tasks it will suffice if you stop by now and then to see how things are going. This method is usually adequate where the job is repetitive and fairly simple. You principally want to make sure that there *is* progress and that everything is going according to plan.

b. *Ask the person to check back with you:* "Joyce, when you're finished with the first five pages, bring them to me to be checked. That way we'll make sure we're on the right track before going too far with the project."

c. *The formal review.* If the task is important and results are not completely predictable, you may want to sit down with the other person and assess what's been accomplished at some halfway point. This is the tack that advertising people sometimes take when they're trying a new ad approach. They'll run an ad in a particular newspaper or magazine and assess the pulling power of a particular layout or copy idea before deciding whether to continue with it or revise it.

Order-giving checklist

Here's a brief set of questions that can help you review your order giving technique and spot weak points, if any.

Notice that these do not merely repeat the Seven Principles, but extend and amplify them. Used in conjunction with the seven basic rules, they'll sharpen your order-giving tools to a fine, effective edge.

Preparation—Are you clear on the facts that will give your order: an objective; direction; a deadline?

Do you make sure that the situation as you have it in mind will coincide with what your subordinate finds when he starts to carry out your order?

Picking the person—All other things being equal, do you give your orders to the subordinate who: will best understand what is to be done; will be most cooperative or have the greatest drive to carry out the order; is capable of the best performance?

Delivery—Do you dish up orders to people in bite-size, digestible portions? Do you get *power* into your orders by delivering them with clarity, calmness, and self-confidence? Do you keep your orders fresh in their minds by using "boosters"—the repeated shots in the arm that help focus attention, such as: reviving their interest; emphasizing goals?

To make your orders stick in general, do you: pin down responsibility? insist on follow-through? fill in for those who require all the details? Do you check progress, either by personal inspection or by having subordinates report back to you?

▶ Recap ◀

Give the highlights of this Chapter a once-over lightly to make them forever yours:

The tool we've been talking about: The art of effective, result-getting order-giving.

How and when to use it: You give instructions or orders or commands whenever people look to you as leader to take charge and tell them what to do. This covers everything from a simple request to a full-fledged program that may involve dozens of people and weeks of effort.

How to develop it: You develop your ability to utilize this high-powered tool for result-getting by incorporating these Seven Principles into your order-giving procedures:

1. Be sure you know the result you want.
2. Prepare the order either in your mind or in writing.
3. Select the right man for the job.
4. Tailor-make your instructions for the person.
5. Suit the order to the situation.
6. Check for understanding.
7. Check for progress.

chapter 10

This chapter attempts what some people say is impossible. You yourself shall be the judge as to whether it succeeds or not.

"It's impossible," a colleague of mine once said, "to make criticism anything but a bitter pill."

"I see it more as a necessary evil," the second member of our little trio chimed in.

Bitter pill? Necessary evil? If either of these statements were true, most of us would be doomed to function at sub-par levels, denied the possibility of improvement.

Fortunately, neither of these negative views of criticism need be true. On the contrary, criticism can be helpful, uplifting. My colleagues were off base, as so many people are, by considering only the common, garden variety of criticism, usually delivered at top voice:

"Ed, how stupid can you get! Didn't I just tell you . . ."

This type of comment isn't criticism at all. It's verbal

**how to
be critical
and be
liked**

127

assault. This chapter tells you how to criticize people, when it's called for, in such a fashion as to make them thankful for it, and to emphasize to all concerned that you have shown yourself to be a perceptive and skillful leader.

This chapter will tell you two things about criticism:

The things *you must not do*, to be effective.

The things *you must do* for your criticism to register successfully, while the person's good will towards you remains either undiminished, or even increases.

Get it straight once and for all

The key distinction to remember in the area of criticism is this:

There are two kinds of criticism. One is destructive and harmful, the other—the kind we'll be talking about here—is constructive, an important highroad to improvement.

The late Arthur Symons, British poet and critic, made the distinction in these words: "I have ever held that the rod with which popular fancy invests criticism is properly the rod of divination; a hazel switch for the discovery of buried treasure, not a birch twig for the castigation of offenders."

Before we get into the specific means by which you can become a master of criticism, an instance from psychiatric lore provides a helpful insight into the reaction to criticism.

A young lawyer's dream

Dr. Erich Fromm, the noted psychiatrist, describes a dream of a young lawyer:

"I saw myself riding on a white charger, reviewing a large troop of soldiers. They cheered me wildly."

Dr. Fromm explained that the day before the lawyer had worked hard on a legal brief. His superior on reading it commented, "I'm really surprised. I thought you would do much better than that."

What did the white horse and the cheering soldiers mean? The interpretation was this: When the young lawyer was a boy he was weak and scrawny. Then he read about Napoleon, a little man whom taller men didn't dare to ridicule. He used to daydream about being Napoleon.

His boss had aroused the same feeling of being jeered at, and unconsciously he fought off this threat by getting on Napoleon's horse and riding at the head of his dream troops.

Of course, the old lawyer couldn't know all this. But if he had worded his criticism to sound less like a judge's verdict, Napoleon's horse would have enjoyed a well earned rest that night.

Inside view of destructive criticism

Psychologists agree that criticism leaves scars on the mind. Physiologists have discovered that it may also make a permanent mark on the body. Doctors have literally seen it happen. For example:

As a result of a necessary operation, a patient was left with a window in his stomach through which reactions could be observed. It was found that whenever he was criticized or felt under attack, "his stomach became red and engorged . . . acid production accelerated sharply and vigorous contractions began."

Criticism is no joke. In the hands of a hostile or unknowing person it can be a club; wielded irresponsibly it can leave its victim emotionally and physically sick.

You nullify all these destructive possibilities by building your criticism according to the hard facts of the individual's sensitivity and his potential for improvement.

To make your comments about people pay off in a desirable fashion, you have to shape them carefully, considerately, constructively.

These rules aren't abstractions thought up by some ivory tower philosopher. They are practical, *they work* because they have been developed from real life situations.

The first thing to bear in mind is the psychological situation into which your criticism is injected.

William G. Shepherd, special consultant to the *Comité International de l'Organisation Scientifique* (CIOS), an international management organization, describes this episode:

"I was about to open the door of a colleague's office when it flew wide open and a girl dashed out. She bumped into me and I was about to mutter the usual apologies when I noticed she was in tears. Before I could say anything she was off down the corridor. Just inside the office door stood a very bewildered executive. He said, 'You sure can't figure some women.' He pointed to a heap of papers on the desk. 'That junk's been lying around for days. I just said it was about time she did a little work around here, and then, as you saw, all hell broke loose.' "

As the bewildered executive discovered, some people are sensitive. We can even go a step further and say that when it comes to criticism, we're *all* super-sensitive.

That wise old man of literature, Somerset Maugham, said, "People ask you for criticism but they only want praise."

It takes a really great man to say and *believe* what Winston Churchill once wrote about himself: "I do not resent criticism even when, for the sake of emphasis, it parts for the time with reality."

Most people want reassurance—not criticism and not honest opinions. But the terrible and wonderful thing about criticism is this—it is a major means for improvement. Nobody improves unless he can spot his faults and find ways to correct them. And both of these flow from effective criticism, criticism of the kind you'll be able to deliver by following the approach developed in the pages ahead.

What's wrong with criticism?

There can be a great deal wrong with criticism—because of the way some people dish it out. It's not only that we all are supersensitive to criticism. The trouble is, well-intentioned but ignorant people add elements to criticism that makes it as explosive as TNT.

A year or so ago I conducted seminars for people in management, from such companies as U.S. Rubber, Remington Rand, and the Chase Manhattan Bank, the sessions sponsored by Cornell University. At one meeting, the discussion focused on the subject of criticism.

"Mr. Uris," one of the managers, a head bookkeeper said, "your TNT idea clears up a great deal of the mystery for me."

"TNT idea?" I queried.

He nodded and pointed to the blackboard on which I had written: Try Not To, had underlined the initial letters, and followed those words by five offenses against effective criticism. What that bookkeeper thus dubbed the TNT idea, has helped enlighten many management groups since. Accordingly, let me introduce you to—

The TNT idea in criticism

The TNT idea takes the dynamite *out* of criticism. How? By pointing out the destructive, even explosive elements that are often mistakenly added. Here are the five Try Not To's that, when incorporated into your approach, defuse criticism of its explosive quality.

Try-not-to #1: misguided kindness

"Anyone can criticize, but it takes a true believer to be compassionate," said a well-known Episcopal minister. In the religious context, certainly compassion rates higher than criticism. However, when in real life criticism is ruled out as being cruel or harmful, you may only be storing up greater headaches for the future. The man, woman, or child, who cannot benefit from constructive criticism simply doesn't exist. Not help, but *harm* is being dealt the individual who is permitted to under-perform or act wrongly without benefit of criticism.

Accordingly, the first Try Not To is: Try Not To indulge in misguided kindness. Don't withhold criticism out of some fancied softheartedness that is more apt to be softheadedness.

Try-not-to #2: bluntness

There's another somewhat opposite destructive approach—*breastbeating bluntness:*

"I'm giving it to you straight from the shoulder," says Ted Trueheart. But chances are he dealt it straight from the shoulder simply because he doesn't know the proper way to do it. As a matter of fact, psychologists tell us this type often has a sadistic streak that betrays itself in this manner. Criticism is more like a healing salve than a bone chisel. Its purpose is to heal and improve not to chip or cut away.

The next of the TNT's is one that is particularly prevalent in marital relationships. The couples that heed this TNT will find marriage a considerably improved state. It applies as well in almost every other kind of human relationship.

Try-not-to #3: nagging

The historical records of Massachusetts tell us that on October 17, 1639, in the town of Salem, one Bessie Sulsgrove, "did get sentenced to the stocks," guilty as charged, of being "a common scold."

Our Puritan ancestors may have been mistaken about a lot of things. Yet they hit it right on the nose when it came to labelling the incessant fault-finder. The designation, "common scold," was a legal accusation that could be made against the overly-active critic, and it was punishable by a spell in the stocks, or one or more descents into a pond on a ducking stool. Not much more need be said about nagging. Don't do it!

Try-not-to #4: getting personal

"You're pretty dumb to pull a boner like that," the inept manager tells his distraught messenger, when the latter had delivered a package to the wrong address.

It's a great temptation to point out a person's faults: he's stupid, slow, lazy, careless, and so on. But let the wisdom of a child point the way.

A psychologist, testing the attitudes of children, asked each of them to write down the names of classmates they liked and didn't like. One child refused to follow instructions. He said, "I like all my classmates, but I don't like everything they do."

The TNT idea here is that you avoid getting personal, that you focus on the *act* you're criticizing, *not* the person.

Avoid any direct reproach that tends to tie an unappetizing label on a person. "How could you be so stupid," will generate nothing but trouble. There's a world of difference between the destructiveness of—

"It was irresponsible of you to handle that yourself," and—

"I can appreciate your wanting to handle it yourself, but when the pressure gets up to that point it's always best to call for help."

Try-not-to #5: accusation

Avoid, both by the tone of your voice and your words, giving the person you're criticizing the idea that you're accusing him of some heinous crime. It's because of this mistaken tack that people become either defensive or resentful.

"What are you doing!" a suburban mother shouts, rushing into the kitchen where her daughter has been trying to mix up some pancake batter. O.K., the kitchen was a mess, some flour had been spilled —a couple of minute's cleanup. But the sense of guilt the thoughtless mother had created in her daughter will linger longer.

Now listen to the approach of an expert critic:

"Some of our best people had trouble learning how to read blueprints," said the foreman of an aircraft assembly department to an employee who had pulled a boner. "But they learned to watch for the following items," etc., etc. The value of this approach is that it avoids telling the man he's unworthy. In fact, at one and the same time you're telling him four different things:

   . . . that he committed an error;

   . . . that the "best people" made the same mistake;

   . . . that they corrected their error and he can too;

   . . . that the way to correct the error is thus and so.

By getting across these points, you provide important foundation stones for improvement.

The TNT idea is half the story of constructive criticism. Add to the five TNT points, four positive elements, and the forging of your tool of criticism is complete. Here are the four positives:

Positive point #1: set the stage

"Praise in public, criticize in private," is one way of stating this important factor. Everybody agrees that criticism ought to be conducted in private. Frequently, a person will admit his error and take helpful correction without feeling he has lost ground in the slightest. But not if it's done in front of an audience!

As important as place is the element of time. For example:

A girl who had been wiring parts has made a major error, which is not discovered until after she has been shifted to winding small armatures. She is just learning her new assignment. Since she will be moved back to wiring next week, should she be told immediately of her error? No. It would only confuse her in the midst of her present learning effort. Wait until that's out of the way, then, when the pressure's off, talk it over.

There's another aspect to timing. The hour of the day may be significant. If you can avoid it, why ruin an employee's digestion by calling him on the carpet just before lunch hour? You're also inviting him to spread gloom among people with whom he eats.

In short, stage your criticism at a time and place that give you maximum receptivity from the other person. Your consideration will help make him more accepting and appreciative of your efforts.

Now, here's the next major element to include in your approach:

Positive point #2: be specific about the error

A young substitute teacher, who probably will not be rehired, walks down the aisles viewing her children hard at work doing Easter baskets. "Very good, Tom," she says, "Oh, Lizzie, that's no good at all," and keeps on walking.

Poor little blond-haired Lizzie is crushed. She knows she's done something wrong, without knowing what to do about it.

Here's a contrast between praise and criticism. In praise, extreme statements may sometimes be useful, even desirable. Never in criticism! Any overstatement of the "that's no good at all" variety gives your target the feeling that you're being unjust. As a result, he'll ignore all your criticism—including the valid part. In short, make certain the person knows exactly what you're criticizing.

Positive point #3: be specific about the remedy

"All right, you'd better get on the ball there." General exhortations of the pep-talk variety leave a lot to be desired. Just consider the difference in effectiveness of these two comments by a baseball coach:

. . . "Get in there an' pitch, boy."

. . . "This batter is a sucker for a fast ball. Put it in high and on the outside."

Spell out just what the person can do to better his performance. This can be the most helpful part of your criticism. After you've suggested a remedy, stay with him. Keep checking his reactions. If he is slow give him more time. Present your corrections step by step.

At least, stay close enough to the situation to make sure that your suggested remedy is the right one and, further, that the other person is able to act on your suggestion.

Positive point #4: follow up

Joseph B. Vandegrift, president of Vandegrift Associates, a management consulting firm retained by some of the country's largest companies, has this to say about this last element in the criticism picture:

"If someone asks me why criticism is often ineffectual, I must answer, because it's seldom followed through. It's easy to put a man on the carpet and forget about him till he pulls another boner. But the manager who really gets mileage out of his criticism is the one who follows it up to make sure he gets improvement."

Vandegrift is not alone in thinking follow-up is the most neglected aspect of criticism. Follow-up shouldn't be haphazard, hit or miss. To be effective, your follow-up should be directed at these results:

1. You want to give the man reassurance, to show that you are really his friend. Do this without making any reference to his past error. Create the feeling that it's not on your mind any more; the error is part of a closed book. You get this idea across by keeping silent about the subject.

2. Give the man an opportunity to ask any questions he may have on his mind, even if it's a simple, "Is this better?" Just being on hand later in the day gives him that chance. If he's timid, he may need some encouragement. Above all, keep your follow-up relaxed.

Remember, the tool works anywhere

The principles we've been talking about will work anywhere. Not only on the job. Try them, and you'll see how effective they are in dealing with your children, your neighbors, fellow club-members.

Used properly, criticism can lead to richer relationships. People will look to you with respect and gratitude for the help they derive from your criticism.

This chapter is entitled How to Be Critical and Be Liked. It's an understatement. Change that Liked to Loved. The sternest, strictest teachers, or superiors in any field, are often the most beloved, because they criticize properly, constructively.

▶ Recap ◀

To get the kind of results from criticism that you devoutly wish, remember the highlights of this chapter:

The tool we've been talking about: criticism, *constructive* criticism.

When to use it: you criticize when people with whom you're associated at work, at home, in your community commit errors which you are in a position to comment on.

How to develop it: You develop your skill at criticizing others and making it a constructive experience all around by following these rules, the five "TNT's" and the four Positive Points:

Try-Not-To #1: Misguided kindness

Try-Not-To #2: Bluntness

Try-Not-To #3: Nagging

Try-Not-To #4: Getting Personal

Try-Not-To #5: Accusation

And now for the four Positive Points—

Positive Point #1: Set the stage

Positive Point #2: Be specific about the error

Positive Point #3: Be specific about the remedy

Positive Point #4: Follow-up

Do these things, and you'll build yourself way up in the respect and esteem of friends, colleagues, subordinates, your family.

chapter 11

You've never heard of the "prevail" technique before because it's been developed especially for this book. It derives from a three-year analysis of the most effective methods of persuasion. Whose methods, you ask? None other than those people who know persuasion as a science, as an art, and as a day-to-day practice—the sales executives of America.

The importance of persuasion

Victor I. Bumagin, director of the Collier-Macmillan Library Service has said, "If I had to pick one key to success in human relations, I would select the ability to persuade. It is the essential quality of that catalyst of the American economy—the salesman. In addition to being the key to salesmanship, any successful attempt to deal with people must feature persuasion. To make people understand, ac-

let the "prevail" technique multiply your powers of persuasion tenfold cept, and follow your viewpoint, is the essence of leadership."

Experts in the human relations field look on persuasion as the opposite of the obsolete bull-of-the-woods approach. There are two ways to get a person to do what you want them to do. One is to do it by weight of your authority or some other pressure tactic. This is a thing of the past. The other is to get him to do it willingly, and this is the function of persuasion.

Former President Eisenhower has pointed out, "Persuasion is the knack of getting people to do what you want done because they want to do it."

A successful example of persuasion ends with the individual willingly undertaking a course of action that you have counseled. This is indeed, as Mr. Bumagin has pointed out, the height of leadership, the ultimate in the mastery of people.

A lot of people feel they have the ability to persuade others and they're dead wrong! For example:

"Persuasion? Sure, I do it every day," one trucking company vice-president asserts. "My people know they either see eye to eye with me, or they're O-U-T."

Even people who don't confuse browbeating with persuasion may mistakenly feel they're masters of the art: "I just persuaded a union delegation to go along with us on the dismissal of a dishonest employee," an industrial relations director of a coffee processor told me proudly. I'd have been more impressed if I hadn't known that the company was completely in the right, and the union group had simply admitted the fact. Persuasion? Not by a long shot.

Master persuasion, and you've got it made

Don't let anyone kid you into thinking persuasion is an easy skill. Those who push that idea seem to think persuasion is made up of 50% softsoap, 25% good intentions, and 25% flimflam.

Let's go along with the 25% good intentions. Certainly you can be more effective when your efforts to persuade are honest and not self-serving. But as for the softsoap or flimflam, the attempt to sell someone your point of view by a verbal fast shuffle—*forget it.*

If persuasion were just a matter of smooth talk, there would be more successful salesmen pulling down salaries and bonuses in six figures. The reason ace salesmen are as rare and as much sought-after as atomic scientists today is that the real art of persuasion requires a thorough, thought-through approach, based on realistic principles. And few men, without the help of a carefully fashioned technique, can make the grade. Remember the bare-handed approach discussed in Chapter 1? You won't find a better example of how useless it is than in the area of persuasion. Nor will you find a better example of the effectiveness of the tool approach than the "prevail" approach to persuasion.

For several years, I participated in the creation of one of the top sales training programs in America, sponsored by the Research Institute of America. This program went to both sales executives and salesmen throughout the United States and Canada.

In my years of studying and writing sales training material, I made a special investigation of the techniques used by salesmen in persuading customers or potential customers to buy what they had to sell.

I studied particularly the methods developed by the most successful companies and the ace salesmen in the field. From this study, eventually emerged the technique I call "prevail."

The "prevail" technique

First I'd like to give it to you fast. The "prevail" technique consists of seven steps. Here they are:

<u>P</u> repare a backlog of good will
<u>R</u> ecognize what he's committed to
<u>E</u> ngross him in your presentation
<u>V</u> isualize the benefits to him
<u>A</u> scertain his objections
<u>I</u> mpel him to re-think his viewpoint
<u>L</u> eave him with an easy decision to make

Here now are the links in the "prevail" method, spelled out in detail:

Prepare a backlog of good will

The Chinese say, "Dig a well before you're thirsty." Your past relationships, if properly developed, are a strong favorable factor in persuading people.

The bigger the backlog of good will you have working for you, the easier for you to gain an agreement. Your efforts at persuasion will begin most auspiciously if you can create a friendly atmosphere. A reputation for honesty and selflessness can also materially assist your efforts.

The importance of friendly contact with the person you are dealing with can be easily illustrated. Assume that a complete stranger stops you on the street and attempts to persuade you to follow a course of action: vote for his candidate, buy his brand of cigarettes, join his club. Your first reaction is likely to be, "Just who is this bird, anyway?" It's normal to want to know something about an individual who sets out to influence us. The more favorable the reputation of the would-be persuader, the stronger is his position.

You don't build this kind of reputation overnight. You acquire it gradually, as a happy by-product of friendliness and fair dealing.

Recognize what he's committed to

This essential point is overlooked again and again in attempts to persuade. Even the experts seem unaware of a simple fact: frequently when we attempt to persuade people we are not working in a vacuum, but rather in an area in which the other person already has done a great deal of thinking, and may even have a well-developed opinion. Here's what I mean:

Dr. William P. Shepard, vice-president of the Metropolitan Life Insurance Company, describes a dramatic instance of attempted persuasion. The setting is a small village in Peru, where the drinking water has been grossly contaminated. Mortality from enteric infections is sky high. However, the problem could be solved if the villagers could be induced to boil their drinking water.

Easy, you'd say. Persuade people to take a simple precaution that would save their lives? No problem.

Yet, after *two years* of effort, a team of competent sociologists and health educators succeeded in persuading only 11 out of 200 village housewives to boil their water.

Why?

The villagers had their own ideas about the meaning of hot and cold. To paraphrase their belief:

"Everybody knows that heat is associated with illness, cold with good health. Boiling water means heat, hence illness, *not* health, as these white people are trying to say."

Perhaps you feel that the mental level of the Peruvian villagers presents a special factor that doesn't apply in other persuasion situations. Well, let's get a little closer to home:

In a small Canadian town, an attempt was made to persuade the populace to enlighten its attitude toward mental illness. Trained field workers applied all the classical methods of health education for six months, *in vain*.

The townspeople tolerated and even joked about mental illness. But once an individual was placed in a mental institution, he was rarely visited, or even spoken of. And in the cases where a patient was discharged, he was heavily stigmatized in the community.

The villagers continued to believe that one must remain aloof from the mentally ill, or run the risk of being suspected of illness oneself.

Remember the old gag, "You can always tell a Harvard student, but you can't tell him much?" The same rule applies for the Peruvians, and the Canadians: they already had firmly established ideas from which they were not readily dissuaded.

It's because of overlooking this important step that the novice salesman often ends up with his foot in his mouth. He goes into a long spiel, trying to sell a prospect Williams' Wonderful Widgets. And as the end of the presentation nears, the prospect leans back and smiles and says, "I'm very sorry, Mr. Smith, but you know we've been using Wampum's Widgets for a number of years and we're perfectly satisfied with them."

As any experienced salesman knows this comment doesn't put an end to the possibility of a sale. But the salesman was wrong not to have discovered in advance the commitment which his prospect has already made in the field of widgets.

The same rule applies in your case. If you're trying to persuade a man to vote for your candidate for the school board, first find out whether he has already selected his own candidate or what his ideas are for a candidate. Then, having ascertained what his commitment is, you know what it is you must *dissuade him from*.

Now comes the next step of "prevail":

Engross him in your presentation

In most sales training material, there is a step which is described by some such phrase as "deliver your presentation" or "give your pitch to the customer."

To me, these are weak words. To "deliver a presentation" signified putting a cut and dried package on the table. That may not get results. What you must do is *engross* your audience in what you have to say. You must capture their interest, force them to concentrate on your words and on your message. Only by getting this type of reaction from your audience are you guaranteed the responsiveness that will help you achieve your objective. Remember, "making your pitch" isn't enough. You want a strong hold on the attention of the person you're persuading.

You engross the other person in what you have to say in a number of ways. First, you make sure that what you have to say is clear and lucidly presented. Whatever the message is, you must state it with forcefulness, with enthusiasm. Let your own belief in your message penetrate to the audience. Illustrate and prove your statements by facts, figures, anecdotes, quotes from qualified individuals.

And now, another step that is little understood outside the sales field, but which is the bread and butter of the expert salesman's approach:

Visualize the benefits to him

In the parlance of the sales trainer, "Don't sell features, sell benefits."

Bernie Carmen, one of the most capable trainers of salesmen in the business, uses an example like this: "There's no point in telling a prospective customer that your product weighs 200 lbs. and stands 6 ft. high, and has a 5 h.p. motor. If he's interested in your machine, it's only because of what it can do for *him*. The features or characteristics of the equipment don't tell him. You have to take one step further. You go from the features to the benefits. For example you might say, 'And this machine weighs 200 pounds, which means, Mr. Customer, that is has extreme stability, and it will sit very solidly on the ground without vibration.' And as far as the height is concerned, you can say, 'And the six-foot height means that it is well within the reach of the average operator. As a matter of fact, even a person below average height can operate our machine easily and that saves money.'"

No matter what message you have to convey, or what you're trying to sell, you must first analyze the thing from the point of view of its benefits. Not what it will do for you, not what it will do for someone else, but *what it will do for the person you are trying to persuade!*

Sometimes the benefit may be stated in terms of money, usually a prime mover. For example, if you were trying to sell something to a businessman, a sure way of getting his signature on your contract is to show him exactly how your product will help him either save or make money.

However, money is not always involved. An ambition realized, for example, may mean more than a sizable amount of cold cash: "Hank, taking this young fellow on as an assistant will be the eventual means of getting you that extended visit to the coast that you've been trying for for the last two years."

In some cases, increased convenience to the other person may be the benefit that will sway him. This appeal is appropriate for the subordinate who must be sold on a new work method, or a top executive whose responsibility it is to O.K. a proposal you're making. One advantage of this type of benefit is that it generally can be spelled out in specifics:

"We could cut down the distance from our warehouse to the point of operation from 520 feet to 270 feet; just think how much power we'd be saving, and how much time we could cut from the total procedure."

In using the idea of benefits, appeal to the normal desires of people: their ambition, their wishes for the future, their pride, their security.

Somewhere in the course of your attempt to persuade the other person, you have to give him the chance to say his piece, to give you some idea of how he's responding to your message. Again, we find that the inexperienced persuader overlooks this critical step altogether. In his overeagerness, he keeps pushing all the time, assuming that the longer he keeps going, the more pressure he's putting on the other person.

In a sense he's right. More pressure *is* building up, but it's building up inside the man, and is more likely to end in an explosion of resentment, rather than in an agreement to follow a course of action. Therefore, the next "prevail" step is:

Ascertain his objections

"I can't afford it," says the housewife to the salesman at the door, knowing that to be a prime discourager. Actually she may have felt the product was too cheap in quality, the color was wrong or she preferred making her purchase of that particular item from her regular dealer.

To spot the reason for resistance to your persuasion attempts, you have to function as a psychologist, a diplomat, a trial lawyer, a keen observer of the expressions, gestures and voice qualities of your fellow man.

"That sounds like an interesting proposal," your boss tells you. "Leave it with me and I'll give it some further thought."

Knowing your superior as you do, you're pretty sure that's the end of your idea. He's just letting you down easy. As you leave his office, you say to yourself, "Now exactly why didn't he go for that plan?"

In any case of persuasion, where you find the going rocky, you must ask yourself that question "What is the basis for resistance?"

You get the answer through discussion, observation, reasoning, or all three. You may try to pin down the resistance by:

. . . asking a direct question: "Now that I've given you the picture pro and con, what's your reaction?"

. . . interpreting the behavior of the other person. You've been trying to get an assistant to change a procedure he's been using. "I don't think it's as good as the way I'm doing it now," he tells you.

You noticed a pained expression on his face as soon as you started talking. You know he hasn't had the opportunity for fair comparison. Therefore you'd probably be correct if you guessed he was exhibiting the normal resistance-to-change syndrome. Here what you must do is to find out *exactly* what his objections to the new method are:

Does he think he'll have his earnings diminished?

Does he think he'll have to work harder?

Does he think the work will be more difficult to keep control of?

Now comes the vital next-to-the-last step. This is:

Impel him to re-think his viewpoint

In this step you sum up, restate, emphasize the key points of your message. You take into account the objections the man may have had to your idea. You also take into account the drawbacks and handicaps, if there are any. By not overlooking the negative aspects of what you're trying to sell him, you make clear your objectivity and your good intentions towards him.

Here is an example of an expert persuader helping another person to re-think a situation. Actually, this dialogue is taken from a presentation made by an ace salesman for an office machine company to a San Francisco office manager:

"Mr. Williams, you've suggested that because it's vacation time, I drop back after Labor Day. I'd be glad to do that, but tell me this. Your company's got salesmen out in the field? Surely you don't expect to hear from them that, since vacations will be starting soon, they won't be sending in any orders for a couple of months. I bet they'd be fired if they did, because your firm is doing everything it can to get business *now*—not next Fall.

"And that's my line. Our proposal is geared to your particular situation here. It'll start adding to your profits immediately. You said a while ago, Mr. Williams, that your budget is completely committed already. I agree that's a serious consideration. But on the other hand, our bookkeeping equipment will help you show immediate savings in reduced costs. In fact, the cost saving is going to show up on your reports the end of the first week. And that's a pretty quick return on your investment, isn't it? In fact, it's the quickest way to *reduce* your budget . . ."

Going back over these last few paragraphs will point up the important elements of the "prevail" step, *Impel him to reconsider his viewpoint:* you take his objections into account, you treat them with respect, advance the information that neutralizes it, and go on to stress *the benefits to him.*

And now comes the wrap-up of the "prevail" technique. It's a final point that makes all the difference between getting the action you want and having that small obstacle remain in the way that may eventually completely block acceptance. Stated simply, the final step is:

Leave him with an easy decision to make

"All you have to do to get the benefits of our service, Mr. Blank, is to sign your name here."

Obviously Mr. Blank is going to have to do considerably more to get the benefits than to put his signature on the dotted line. He is going to have to lay out a number of dollars, do without other things he might have bought for his money.

But the expert persuader invites an easily accomplished act that is *symbolic of agreement*. Note another example of easing the road to agreement:

A top real estate salesman specializing in industrial properties in Rockland County, New York, told me of this incident. He had been trying to get a busy executive to view an out-of-town lot. He told the potential customer of the advantages of the property, stated its attractive price, and so on. He concluded his efforts with, "Just let me know when it's convenient for you to see the parcel, Mr. Frank, and I'll be glad to drive you over."

But with this injunction, he had asked the executive to do a great deal—to perform a complicated procedure involving, among other things, a decision as to whether viewing the property deserved a higher priority than a dozen other items on his daily schedule.

One day the real estate man pushed the right button: "Mr. Frank," he said over the phone, "I don't think you should put off seeing the property any longer. I'll have my car right outside the door of your home tomorrow morning. We can get out to see the lot and I'll have you back at your office at your regular starting time."

I'll have the car right outside your door . . .

Getting an individual to go along with the first step usually signifies success. Removing the obstacles from the first step, making it simple and convenient has always been, and will always be, a key to maximum effectiveness in persuasion.

And so you "prevail."

▶ RECAP ◀

The tool: the "prevail" technique of persuasion.

When to use it: whenever you want to sway an individual or group to your viewpoint, or to take an action you feel is desirable.

How to sharpen it: practice these steps, *all* of them:

<u>P</u> repare a backlog of good will
<u>R</u> ecognize what he's committed to
<u>E</u> ngross him in your presentation
<u>V</u> isualize the benefits to him
<u>A</u> scertain his objections
<u>I</u> mpel him to re-think his viewpoint
<u>L</u> eave him with an easy decision to make

Part III

Build People for
Superlative Results

chapter 12

This chapter is about training —the development of people. Training is a truly amazing process. You take a bit of yourself and implant it in the mind of another person and it grows and becomes a part of him, making him a better, more capable individual. He then becomes worth more to himself and more to you.

While the process may seem to verge on the mystical, it certainly doesn't seem to be controversial. Why should anyone knock training? Yet, the fact remains that many people are down on training. Meet some of them:

. . . *wised-up Willie.* He knows it all already. No one, he thinks, can teach him anything. Why waste time?

. . . *nervous Ned.* He says, "If they try to train me, it means I'm not good enough as I am . . ."

. . . *hopeless Hanna.* "I just can't do any better than I'm doing now."

. . . *close-to-the-vest Vincent.* He's an example of a

increasing
their ability
to deliver

man *in authority* who feels the way to stay in power is to hold every-body else down. Training? Of course not. Let's not make people any smarter, they might start getting ideas.

Developing people's abilities, knowledge, or understanding isn't an easy job. Furthermore, as we've just indicated, some people fear that it may arouse negative reactions. Then why does anyone bother?

Thomas J. Watson, Jr., head of the giant International Business Machines Corporation, knows one answer. Back in 1956 he became aware of a serious executive shortage that threatened the company's growth. He set the wheels in motion that would produce the necessary training to "help men grow as executives." In his case, training was a prerequisite for company growth.

The top management of General Electric has spent millions of dollars to increase the abilities of its employees, from the lowest echelons on to the highest. The steam behind this effort was GE's desire to improve as an organization. This could not be achieved unless thousands of employees could be trained to do better in their jobs or to qualify for promotion.

Organizations of every kind have educational programs to enlarge the horizons or capabilities of their members.

In your own case, you'll find many reasons and many occasions for teaching:

As a parent, you repeatedly find it necessary to teach your child—everything from table manners to some of the philosophical niceties of living.

As a youth leader at a "Y" or for a Scout troop, you'll find the occasion to teach woodcraft, handicrafts, nature lore.

Community living abounds with occasions for passing along your know-how to others. You teach a neighbor how to pour cement or make a cabinet. You may want to teach a willing but inexperienced friend some skill, such as publicity writing to further the ends of an organization to which you both belong. You may want to teach a youngster tennis, swimming, skiing.

Every group has the problem of fund raising. If you are expert in this field, your ability to teach others what you have learned can make a major difference to the success of your group's fund drive.

And of course, there's no need to elaborate on the endless occasions for training that exist on the work scene. Whether you want to teach a new secretary the department's filing system or prepare an

assistant to take over part of your responsibility, the more effective
your training, the more successful the end results.

Can teaching be tough? listen . . .

Anyone who thinks teaching is a breeze is kidding himself. Talk
to school teachers. Brooklyn-born Emanuel Fineberg teaches in Har-
lem's P.S. 68, a special service school because all its pupils are hardship
cases. There seems to be no end product to Fineberg's work. The best
he hopes for is that a handful of children will be influenced by him,
and that to many more he will be fondly remembered as "Mr. Fineberg."

Yes, teaching occasionally seems unrewarding. It may even be
hazardous! An incident that took place in Stockport, England, makes
the point. According to the *Associated Press* dispatch:

> A policeman saw 65-year-old spinster Margaret Hunter alone in a
> car bearing 'L' plates, indicating she was learning to drive and should
> be under supervision. She told the constable: "I had an instructor with
> me. But when I stopped at the traffic signal he jumped out of the car
> shouting, 'It's lunacy! It's suicide! I'm not going another inch with you
> driving.'"

Aside from its related difficulties, however, teaching is tough because it's a rare skill to master. Amazingly few people are really good
teachers. Adequate? Yes. Outstanding? No. You'll learn why in the
next paragraphs.

The easy target—and the tough one

Probably no other subject in management literature has gotten as
much coverage as training. Supervisors are taught how to train. As a
matter of fact, during World War II, the U.S. government conducted
a mammoth program whose sole object was to train supervisors to train
employees—the famous "J" projects—Job Instruction Training, Job
Relations Training, and so on.

Executives are taught how to develop their subordinates, often
assisted by experts from the Personnel Department. They may cover
anything from how to write a report to how to deal with a customer.

Almost every company of appreciable size has a training or development program of some type going all the time.

As a result of this concentration on training, dependable, time-tested rules have been pretty well developed. You'll get a quick run-through of the basic steps of ordinary training. *But these are only the minimum steps you need to know!* It is the purpose of this chapter to go light years beyond the principles of routine training. The few rules you need to achieve the ordinary teaching goals without a hitch can be simply stated, and will be. However, after giving you these basic principles of training, we'll go on to tell you how to become an outstanding trainer, a one-in-a-hundred teacher who gets superb results.

"The good is the enemy of the better"

There's a great deal of wisdom in the old French proverb that suggests that often, people achieve a get-by level, then stop. In many cases, if you can do something adequately, there is no incentive to go beyond that to become outstanding. However, in the area of training, the difference between being an adequate teacher and being a standout can be tremendous. Listen to the raves of a student exposed to superior teaching:

Wrote a Harvard undergraduate in his diary in the year 1875: "At last, it's happened. I have one really inspiring teacher, Professor William James. His lectures on psychology change the whole world for me. He has the ability to make learning the most exciting experience of my entire college career."

How does a teacher ever get to be that good? To a large extent, the answer can be summed up in the one word: *rapport*—a special relationship with your pupil, the one that will make you the kind of teacher that people never stop praising, one who increases the skill and understanding of others, to everyone's pleasure and profit.

Take care of the preliminaries

To make your training effective, you have to get straight on a few arrangements about the sessions you'll hold. True, they're details, but worth your attention:

Formal or informal? Informal training is generally unscheduled. You simply fit it in as the opportunity arises. Formal training, on the other hand, may require a special place or conditions that have to be arranged. For example, the "field trip" usually figures in formal teaching. It's all very well to chat with your child about ancient Egypt. But if you want the subject to sink in, you may take him to see the mummies and relics at the museum.

Where and when? Spell out the best time and place. Aim for surroundings that are relatively quiet and uncluttered. "I started showing my neighbor how to cut a dress pattern," one housewife relates ruefully. "Between my baby and the telephone, we had six interruptions in the first half hour. She left in a huff and I don't blame her!" Interruptions, distractions get in your way. Plan accordingly.

What size portions? Will the training be more effective in one 5-hour session or five 1-hour sessions? Individual ability to absorb is a factor. Plan your sessions according to the difficulty or "meatiness" of the subject and the learning speed of your student.

Group or individual? Whether you give individual or group instruction depends on the time available and what's being taught. Naturally, if you can teach several at the same time, you multiply your efficiency. But avoid getting the group so large that it becomes unruly or difficult for you to retain the "personal touch."

The basics of training

These are the four steps you must know and follow to make your teaching get through to your "students," the ABC's of teaching that help you achieve the important day-to-day goals of training:

1. *Be sure you know the subject you want to teach.* It's a good rule and should always be followed. Occasionally a person tries to fake it, and confusion takes over.

And take a tip from the pros. Don't try to be a Mr. Memory. Backstop yourself with notes, handbooks, reference material that you can fall back on, if necessary.

2. *Break the subject down into elements.* Let's say you're going to teach someone how to play tennis. First, you'll explain the general rules of play. Then you might begin a session of training on forehand strokes, then backhand. Finally, you'll explain about delivering the service.

Almost every job, skill or craft consists of a number of related activities. By isolating each of these, teaching them separately, you usually can prevent the kind of bewilderment that sets in when the attempt is made to put over the whole ball of wax at one time.

3. *Have the trainee perform.* No one ever learned to swim by watching someone else do it. Learning by doing is effective because it gets the skill into the brain and muscles of the trainee. Some jobs—for example, operating an office copier—require a relatively brief run-through. Others—for example, running a desk-top calculator—may require weeks.

4. *Follow up on the training sessions.* You want to make sure that the teaching has "taken." Check both the learner's methods and the result of the operation. If you've been teaching someone how to model in clay, for example, you would want to both observe how the student goes about the work, and then evaluate the product of his efforts.

Also in question here is the question of how long your pupil retains what you've taught. As Mark Twain once said, "My memory is good, but my forgettery is outstanding."

People *do* forget, and scientists have been interested in finding out how quickly. Researchers have recently come up with some startling figures that show how fast our learning disappears if we don't keep at it:

Interval	Percent Forgotten	Percent Retained
⅓ hour	42	58
1 hour	56	44
8 ¾ hours	64	36
1 day	66	34
2 days	72	28
6 days	75	25

As Confucius might say: "If they don't keep practicing, don't be surprised if they forget what they once knew well."

It's important that you *don't* assume that since your explanation has been clear, and the student is intelligent, results are guaranteed.

Above all, don't depend on a student's *common sense.* Common sense is far from common, as this story from India will show:

The wife of the principal of the Mission College, in Allahabad, India, hired a Hindu carpenter to repair a window frame that was badly rotted. She drew a little sketch to show the man how it was to be done and went off elsewhere in the house. When she came back an hour later, she found that the carpenter had made a mess of it. Naturally, the lady was exasperated. When the carpenter explained that he had tried to follow instructions, she said: "But why didn't you use your common sense?" The Hindu pulled himself up to his full height and said: "But common sense, madam, common sense is a gift of God; I have technical knowledge only."

The four basic steps

In those four steps you have the basics of training:
Be sure you know the job you want to teach.
Break the job down into elements.
Have the trainee actually perform.
Follow up on your training to make sure that it's taken.

These points, carefully followed, will put you on a par with most of the qualified developers of people in business and industry. Now, let's go on to the more ambitious objective, that of making you an *outstanding* developer of people.

The road to superiority

Remember at the outset, you have *two* reasons for wanting to train people. One may be a practical, even a selfish reason. For example, you may want to teach your youngster how to run the power mower so that you can get out from under the chore. But no matter how mundane the lesson, how practical the purpose, remember this: *Any time you teach a person anything you're improving him as a person, as well as increasing his capabilities.* The outstanding teacher is the one who has a real interest in bettering his students, in making them not only smarter and more capable people, but *better* people.

The elements that go to make up the great teacher can be incorporated into your approach to teaching. These are the kinds of things you add to your teaching technique:

1. *"Adopt" the other person.* The really effective teacher has a warm and paternal feeling for his pupils. This doesn't mean he develops a condescending attitude. It's altogether possible to have a benevolent

and paternal feeling towards a student without implying superiority. This feeling of warmth in the good teacher becomes fused with the sincerity he imparts in his teaching.

2. *Get to know him better than he knows himself.* You're off to a good start when you understand the person you're trying to teach, know what makes him tick. If he's a stranger or someone you know only slightly, take some time to chat. Talk about his interests, ambitions, hopes. Give him a chance to talk about the subject of your teaching.

This type of talk does something for him and something for you. It relieves him of the nervousness everybody feels with the process of learning. At the same time, it gives you the opportunity to see how intelligent, how quick and how experienced he is. All this knowledge you use for the next step, pacing your teaching to his capacity to absorb.

3. *Tailor your teaching to his needs.* The expert trainer recognizes that each learner is different. Some catch on fast, others are slow. Some understand immediately when you give a verbal explanation. Others will learn twice as fast when you show or demonstrate the information.

Remember that as tough as *teaching* is, *learning* is usually tougher.

Beginners always find learning painful and fatiguing.

There's a surefire antidote for this reaction. As Gilbert Highet points out in his book on the art of teaching: "Few things will diminish the difficulty and fatigue like the kindness and patience of a good teacher."

4. *Take the time to get him relaxed.* Movie star Cary Grant was recently interviewed in his suite in the Hotel Plaza, by Miss Sidna Brower, of the *New York World-Telegram & Sun.* At least, Mr. Grant was supposed to be interviewed, but like the experienced hand he is, he took over:

He pulled his chair up to Miss Brower and said, "Uncross your legs."

"Beg your pardon?"

"Uncross your legs," he repeated. "You are too tense and nervous."

Miss Brower obeyed.

"Close your eyes and breathe deeply," he said.

Miss Brower did as directed.

Mr. Grant explained, "The best actor is the most relaxed actor; the best boxer is the most relaxed boxer. Even on the subway, we can close our eyes and take a deep breath to relax."

Mr. Grant's dictum on relaxation applies in spades during the learning process. However, telling people to relax is not the only way to put people at ease. A quiet tone in your voice, an easy friendly manner, help. And if appropriate, humor can be especially effective. The wise teacher knows that 45 minutes of study with 5 minutes of laughter is worth twice as much as 50 minutes of straight instruction.

Humor has an additional worthwhile effect: when individuals laugh together, they cut down the artificial barriers between teacher and learner. Humor creates a bond which makes teaching easier.

5. *Encourage, encourage, and then encourage some more.* The prevailing mood of most learners is one of uncertainty and self-doubt: "I don't think I can do that," says the young man who's being told to crouch in the water with the points of his water-skis pointed forward.

"Sure you can," says the water-ski instructor, helps him get into the start position and rewards the self-doubting youngster by warm words of praise. Very often the teacher's encouragement is the only antidote for the crushing effects of preliminary failure.

The housewife teaching her daughter how to bake a pie is confronted by her pupil staring in dismay at a charred flattened mess inside a pie tin.

"Guess I just wasn't cut out to be a baker," says the downhearted teenager. "Nonsense," assures her mother, "you should have seen my first attempt. Tomorrow we'll try it once more and this time . . ."

And as important as praise and reassurance are, you can encourage people to stick with it, to maintain their efforts in additional ways. For example, keeping the learning experience fresh and stimulating is sometimes accomplished by showing your trainee a new angle, or passing along a few more sophisticated tricks of the trade.

John E. Lane, of Union, South Carolina, whose management experience has put him in position to know, has said: "Allowing a trainee to stagnate on part of a job when he is capable of handling the whole operation will very often result in slowing his pace." Acting on Lane's hint means that, as you think it appropriate, you push out the limits of the teaching area, help the learner raise his sights.

6. *Expect the road to be bumpy.* It's important to know that the learning process has ups and downs. It was the late Dr. William Bryan, formerly president of Indiana University, who first called attention to fluctuations in learning. Dr. Bryan found out that:

. . . learning does not progress smoothly. There are good and bad periods.

. . . learning is faster during the first few practice sessions, then tends to slow down.

. . . there is often a "plateau" in learning, a time when the learner does not improve noticeably. He may even get worse! It's at this point that the trainee becomes discouraged and it's your job to provide a lift, a restimulation of self-confidence so that he can go on improving.

Willis Whitney, Research Director of the General Electric Co., has said, "Many learners have found they get there just about the last time before giving up."

7. *Have a graduation ceremony.* Not formal, of course, but check out the trainee when you've finished the teaching and your "pupil" has apparently finished the learning.

There are some last final checks to be made:

. . . have the trainee run through the job. Have him tell you before he performs each step what he is going to do next. See if he knows how he will do it and why he thinks it should be done that way.

. . . check his knowledge and understanding of what he's been taught. Together, evaluate his performance and the quality of the job he turns in.

Your greatest satisfaction as a trainer comes when the trainee can stand on his own two feet. Aside from the fact that the work gets done better, there's his increased skill. In addition, there's a feeling of permanent payoff about the time and effort expended.

Let these words of philosopher John Dewey be your greatest reward: "A good teacher affects the future. He never can tell where his influence stops."

▶ RECAP ◀

To skim the cream off this chapter, here are the key points to remember:

The tool: teaching, training, developing the skills and understanding of others—friends, neighbors, your family, fellow club members, or people in your company.

When to apply it: whenever there's a need for knowledge; when-

ever somebody says, "Can you teach me how . . . "; when you want
to help somebody get ahead, or improve himself either in general or
particular; finally, when you yourself feel the urge to impart something of yourself to another as a kind of psychic philanthropy.

Keys you use to master the tool: here's how to go about training:
The preliminaries: decide on these details:

Formal or informal?

Where and when?

What size portions?

Group or individual?

The 4 basic steps: follow these ABC's:

1. Be sure you know the subject you want to teach.
2. Break the subject down into elements.
3. Have the trainee perform.
4. Follow up on the training sessions.

And now, for the secret of superiority in teaching, the seven rules
that will make you an outstanding trainer:

1. "Adopt" the other person.
2. Get to know him—better than he knows himself.
3. Tailor your teaching to his needs.
4. Take the time to get him relaxed.
5. Encourage, encourage, and then encourage some more.
6. Expect the road to be bumpy.
7. Have a graduation ceremony.

chapter 13

The date was March 31, 1962. The occasion was the last meeting of a course, "How to Handle the Problem Employee," I had been giving to a management group in New York City. Cornell University, the sponsor of the sessions, had provided certificates for the enrollees. At the close of the evening, I dutifully handed out the "diplomas" to the 30-odd managers from a broad range of companies who made up the group.

Last in line was Philip Russell, who accepted his certificate with a brief word of thanks. But later he came up to me:

"Mr. Uris," he said, "I want you to know that this course has been the most eye-opening experience of my entire career. I had my doubts about it at first. But in learning about dealing with the problem employee, I learned more about management, more about people, and more about myself, than by anything else I ever studied."

how to solve problem people

You probably thought this chapter was going to take up the question of what you can do for the "problem child," the thorn-in-the-side individual.

You're perfectly correct. That's at least *half* of what this chapter's about. However, in addition to this highly worthwhile goal, the rewarding experience that Phil Russell described will also be yours.

Learning how to deal with the problem child is a kind of postgraduate course in human relations. You master new and exacting skills to cope with the problem individual. In acquiring these skills, you broaden immeasurably your powers to manage people in general. As Phil Russell did, you'll gain rich insights into behind-the-scenes factors that make a group click, that make certain individuals behave as they do, and finally, and perhaps most important, you become aware of your own reactions to some tough and demanding situations. As you learn to convert the destructive, recalcitrant, couldn't-care-less individual into a helpful, worthwhile contributor, your power to manage people will grow beyond your most optimistic expectation!

The problem child can bring on nightmarish situations. And our progress in technological areas, our growing dependence on the machine, increases rather than decreases the threat. Here's the shape of the future, as described by a man to whom the future is of everyday concern—Robert W. Sarnoff, Chairman of the Board of the National Broadcasting Company:

> Instruments of scientific and industrial revolutions are multiplying our control over nature to an extent that defied prophecy only a generation ago. Today, $20 billion a year is being invested in research and development in the United States. While nearly three-quarters is provided by the government, the bulk of the work is being done within industry and the resulting advances in technology are spreading throughout the economy, both public and private.

As many people are becoming aware, the machine giants Mr. Sarnoff describes are under the control of people. Talk about a bull in a china shop! Let one person go haywire in a modern office or plant and tremendous losses may result. The more complicated the system, the more vulnerable it is to foul up or destruction. A gay Hollywood comedy, "That Touch of Mink," starring Doris Day and Cary Grant, makes the point.

Midway through the movie Miss Day gets a temporary job as a

file clerk in an electronic data-processing center. She goes berserk, and flings drawersful of punchcards over the office. The audience loves it. But the manager of one such center confided, "It could happen. And if it did, it would take weeks to straighten out the mess."

Problem people demand your attention because they are potential wreckers. They can ruin friendships, they can cause serious rifts in previously stable organizations. Permitted to go about their willful way, the best of plans can blow up in your face.

Every company, every department, every group or organization is seldom without one or more problem members.

Few people are clear on what to do about them.

Even the experts are confused. Read what some of them say and you get the idea that the problem individual is a non-conformist, an offbeat individual who speaks, thinks or acts differently from others in his group. Or, according to some, he's a neurotic, maladjusted individual.

The plain fact is, an individual might be any of these, *and still not be a problem*.

Regardless of what some of the experts may try to tell you, there's one and only one quality that makes an individual a problem to others. It's this: he causes *damage* or *harm*. If there is no damage, *regardless of appearances*, or *behavior*, then you're not dealing with a problem person. Once you understand and master this one fact, you're in much greater command of the whole subject of dealing with the problem person than half the managers and personnel executives in the business.

Identifying the problem individual

Know what to look for and it's easy to spot the problem person. Let's take a down-to-earth instance, a person we quickly can agree is a problem. Who shall it be? Let's select the kind of problem person that occurs all too frequently on the work scene—the careless, indifferent employee. Note the three ways in which he causes loss or damage:

1. *He underperforms in his job*. He produces less work than he's supposed to, or turns out excessive amounts of bad work. One way or another, he fails to measure up to the performance standards set for him.

2. *He interferes with the performance of others*. Take our careless worker, for example. Since he has a couldn't-care-less attitude, he's a constant source of annoyance and interference. Squabbles arise, and

often as not, he's at the bottom of them. "How do you expect me to do my work properly," a co-worker of Kid Careless says, "when half the pieces he gave me have been improperly drilled?"

3. *He causes harm to his group.* Few things damage a group's reputation as much as having one of its members get into trouble. That's why colleges must do such a stern policing job of its students. That's why some organizations have such strict membership requirements.

Getting back to our Kid Careless, he can do harm to his company in several ways. First of all, there's the possibility that his sloppy work will get into the hands of a customer, draw a complaint, a cancellation, or even a complete break. As the customer might tell the Kid's employer: "We have no intention of doing business with a company that delivers under-par products."

And indifferent employees like Kid Careless, particularly when they work in contact with outsiders, do violence to a company's public image. Just remember your impression of the last firm you phoned in which an unpleasant telephone operator made you feel as though you were invading her privacy by bothering her with your call.

The three-point test

Get clear on the basic quality that distinguishes a problem individual—*he causes harm or damage.* Lord knows, there are a great many people in this world of ours who have peculiarities. Einstein liked to dress like an undergraduate beatnik; Sir Isaac Newton kept apples in his rooms till they rotted and the place smelled like a cider mill; Hedda Hopper insists on wearing barn-sized hats. Yet, eccentricities like these do not make the people who sport them, problems!

Coming closer to home, we can say that the man or woman in your group who is a non-conformist—for example, he may dress differently, or have some interests that are unique—is not the kind of person to be classified as a "problem child."

You can pin down the identity of the problem individual firmly, eliminating all doubt. You need only pose three simple questions to get a clear and positive answer. Ask these questions and you can establish beyond the shadow of a doubt whether an individual does or doesn't belong in the problem category:

Is he causing loss or damage?

Is the loss or damage likely to persist?

Is there no simple solution?

If the answer in each case is *yes*, the individual under consideration is indeed a problem and requires your special attention, if you have any responsibility in the case.

Handling the problem person

In what we suggest now, we make one assumption. It is that you're the problem employee's superior or the problem child's parent or a responsible official of a group or club to which the problem person belongs—in short, that you're in a position to take action.

Once you're sure in your own mind that *a*. the person is indeed a problem, and *b*. you are responsible, here are the steps you can take:

1. *Weigh the gains and losses.* "Old John is a drag on the whole operation," the head librarian of a suburban Philadelphia library told me, "but we feel we can sacrifice a little efficiency for the sake of sentiment. You see, he was one of the founders of the place."

A businessman, head of a Long Island lumber yard, made the point about retaining an old employee who had become a problem because of ill health: "Tom's arthritis represents a real handicap, but because of his loyalty, we feel we'll just have to add that loss to the cost of doing business."

In some cases, companies trying to cope with a problem employee have taken a stand, only to find it embarrassingly necessary to backwater, reverse a decision. Here's one that the top echelons of a Pennsylvania steel fabricating company still wince over:

The company took on a man as shipping clerk who flopped on the job from the first day. He had trouble mastering procedures, failed to follow the simplest instructions. After giving the man half a dozen warnings, the shipping supervisor decided to let the man go.

It was a fair but unfortunate decision. The employee's war record and civic activities gave him considerable personal popularity in the community. The clamor that arose at the dismissal reached top management's ears:

"We were wrong to put the man in that job in the first place," said the company president. "In a sense, we're responsible for the failure and we must try to place him in another spot." The dismissal was revoked.

The moral of the story is, there may be circumstances about a problem person that prevent you from doing what comes naturally. The person is a problem *precisely because you can't take the obvious or logical action!*

In short, you must decide whether the problem is one you must live with because of extenuating circumstances, or proceed to the next phase of the procedure:

2. *Ask yourself, "What can be changed?"* Before you act, you want to consider what the possibilities are. If there's to be any relief, something's got to give. What can it be? Generally, there are three ways out:

. . . *behavior.* The perennial late-comer in many cases can be "cured" by making it clear that he must conform to the same rules that others do. In many cases you can persuade a man to alter what he's doing and conform to the required standard of conduct. Many supervisors report that a single warning is sufficient to improve a poor attendance record, stop destructive horseplay, or put an end to careless habits around dangerous machines.

. . . *attitude.* The club member who causes trouble by carrying a chip on his shoulder may have his pugnacity watered down, if you can help him see that his attitude is self-defeating: "Tom, you'd find people are much friendlier if you'd just let them show it. If you'd stop trying to turn every disagreement into an argument and every argument into a fight, you'd end up being one of the most popular people in the whole group."

Other harmful attitudes that you often can modify: the man who's "never wrong," the over-dependent individual; the girl who's "too popular." Toward the end of this chapter you'll find a gallery of problem children that includes attitudes like these, with tips on how to handle them.

. . . *situation.* Sometimes you find the problem child *is* one because of a situation in which he has become enmeshed. Here's a thumbnail case history that makes the point:

Edwin Thorpe, a programmer in a Los Angeles electronic data processing center, changed almost overnight from a tractable and pleasant person to one who was recalcitrant and insubordinate. His boss eventually discovered the reason. Another programmer had been hired at a higher salary than Ed was drawing. Once the facts in the case emerged and the justice of Ed's claims became clear, salaries were rectified and peace descended on the programming room.

Notice what happened: a *situation* changed a perfectly good employee into a problem. His superior learned what the situation was and, by dealing with it, was able to change the problem child back to the "normal" category. This is the general pattern for coping with the "situational" problem child.

What you can't change

Nowhere has it been suggested that you attempt to change a man's personality, or the kind of person he basically is. You can change behavior or attitude. But don't try to convert a slow, thoughtful person into a back-slapping extrovert, or vice versa. And don't think for a minute that you're going to take a tense, nervous person and change him by saying, "Relax." The odds are tremendous, and all against you.

We know that sometimes people do seem to change. *But*—there's a "but" to such changes. Usually, when individuals change, you'll see that it's because they're young and have the flexibility to adapt or the transformation is not so much an alteration of personality as it is the development of an area of personality that existed before, *but was hidden or latent.*

Accept Lincoln's wisdom: "God grant me the patience to accept what cannot be changed, the courage to change what should be changed, and the wisdom to know one from the other."

3. *Don't make his problem your problem.* It's a trap you must side-step, because once in it, there's no escape: avoid getting trapped in the problem child's personal affairs!

It happens too often. A well-meaning leader listens to a problem individual's tale of woe: "I'm absent so often, Mr. Smith, because of illness at home. My old mother . . ." etc., etc.

Of course, you have to use your judgment. In some cases, there are explanations that you must take into account. But even though you sympathize with the person, avoid having him dump his problem on your shoulders.

True, illness at home may explain poor attendance, or undependable transportation may explain frequent lateness. But on the job or off, if an individual has a responsibility to be present at a given place at a given time, he must make whatever arrangements are necessary. It's *his* responsibility! Other people have sick dependents at home, and take the steps necessary to have them taken care of.

A supervisor told me: "One of my hand finishers used traffic jams as his explanation for coming in late. I knew for a fact that the traffic was terrible, and I accepted the excuse until it suddenly dawned on me that four or five other people came to the plant by exactly the same route. And *they* always checked in on time."

Once you show a willingness to make the other person's problem your problem, you've opened a Pandora's box of troubles. The sad fact is, by encouraging the person's dependence, you make him *less* responsible and *less* capable of coping with his difficulties.

Your strongest move to take an individual out of the problem category is to make him aware of his responsibilities and the need to live up to them. *Then*, by helping him shoulder his own burden rather than carrying it for him, you assist him in an area in which he *really* needs help—the development of his ability to deal with his problem.

4. *Tell him the truth about his position.* When you deal with a problem individual, there is a final alternative to be considered. On the job, it may be dismissal or demotion. In a club or organization, it may mean a move to terminate his membership.

Even in a neighborhood situation, where no formal organization is involved, there may be an ultimate penalty—the disfavor of other neighbors.

For some problems, the final alternative may be the law. For instance, one residential neighborhood in Westchester suffered from the incursions of two huge dogs, the beloved pets of one of the local citizens. Pleas from her neighbors that the animals be kept on a leash brought only refusal. The dog lover accused her neighbors of being cruel to animals, of being heartless, inconsiderate, and so on.

When reminded that her dogs had frightened children, upset garbage cans, torn clothing from clothes lines, the lady denied or belittled all that was said.

Finally, one of the neighbors made the case clear: "We've put up with a great deal of inconvenience and hardship and downright loss because of your dogs. The next time they appear off the leash, we're going to report you to the police."

No leader uses the ultimate threat lightly. On the work scene, for example, you certainly don't threaten dismissal without considerable forethought. But once you've gone through the first three steps recommended here, and weighed the gains and losses, you know what to do. You know the extent of the damage the individual has caused, you know how strong to make the warning.

In dealing with the problem individual, however, remember that you may be dealing with more than *one* person. In a community situation, you may be fighting for the survival of a worthwhile civic group, or the peace of mind of other individuals. Friends, family, fellow workers may be involved. All these people, their interests and reactions should be taken into account as you consider your moves.

A gallery of problem children
—and how to handle them

The toolkit provided in the previous pages arms you for any problem child that may come your way. To still further pin down your approach, to give you a closeup of specific cases, here are some problem people who typically upset the applecart. Study them and you'll still further equip yourself to handle difficult or explosive human relations with a sure and confident touch.

Perfect Pete. His theme song: "Of course, I admit when I'm wrong. But I'm never wrong."

This joker knows it all. And he may not say so in so many words, but he feels he's beyond correction or improvement. How does he cause loss? He riles others, makes errors and refuses to be confronted by the consequences.

He'll twist the facts into a pretzel to make the point that an error which leads to a cash loss is an "investment in the future"—though he may have a bit of trouble in explaining *whose* future or what the investment is in.

As is true for all problem children, you haven't the time, the inclination, or the license to psychoanalyze him. You consider steps like these:

1. Let him know it's no crime to make mistakes. "We all go wrong every once in a while—*even the best of us.*"

2. Avoid unnecessary criticism. He's likely to be especially supersensitive.

3. When necessary, don't criticize *him*, but the *method* he used. "Next time, let's try a different procedure. I think it will work out better."

4. Build his self-respect when he does an outstanding job. Then he'll have less need of this phony defensive shell.

Uncertain Merton. "Mr. Jones, I just wanted to ask you . . ."

Male or female, this type of person is a Clinging Vine. He deserves your pity rather than your blame. Past events have undercut his self-confidence, made him overly-dependent on others.

It takes time to get the unsure or overly cautious individual to stand on his own two feet. But if you want him off yours:

1. Provide reassurance rather than information. This doesn't mean that you withhold information he may need to act. But if experience is any guide, chances are, Merton usually has the answer to most of his questions before he asks them.

2. Keep his assignments on the easy and simple side, not permanently, but until he can nourish the puny little plant of his self-confidence to reasonable health.

3. Keep feeding the ball back to him. When he does get into deep water, help him figure his own way out. Try to make him see that he *does* have the answer: "How do you think it should be handled?"

4. Use reverse consultation. Let him participate in minor decision-making. Then, build him up to more important matters—consult *him* on decisions you have to make, for example.

5. Extend his ability to take on tougher tasks. Use each successful accomplishment as a springboard for a slightly harder assignment. Be ready to assist, but give him full credit for achievement. Every once in a while remind him of how far he's come: "A year ago, Merton, you'd have had a lot of trouble putting that deal across. Today you did it in a breeze."

Optimistic Otto. "Let's look at the bright side . . ."

For most people, optimism is a doorway to success—but for him, it's an escape hatch from failure. His errors are made to be shrugged off, not mended.

Remember the gag? "Stop complaining. Things could be worse. So I stopped complaining, and things got worse—much worse."

This joke was made to order for Otto. He's the one whose protection against failure is rose-colored glasses.

Behind his attitude is a considerable degree of irresponsibility based on immaturity. And if you resolve to let nature take its course, he may try to kid you along indefinitely. To effect a real change in his viewpoint, you have to plan a careful, continuing campaign.

Try working along these lines:

1. Start by putting solid ground underfoot. Stress the *importance* of each of his assignments at the outset plus the *necessity* for success.

2. Tighten up on the reins in the course of his work. Have him *report back* to you on progress.

3. Bring other group members into the act. When his slap-happiness interferes with *their* work, stand back; let *them* tell him the score.

4. Take your final leaf out of *his* book. Show him that you, too, can be optimistic: "O.K., let's look at the bright side—by making sure there is a bright side, next time." And then go on to suggestions that will prevent a second failure.

Too-gentle John. "Tom says we ought to . . ."

You may know someone like the historical John Alden, who prefers to speak for others. He'll tell you, "Bill thinks thus-and-so." His failure to advance his own interests can cost you information, ideas, and a valuable point of view. And, of course, it's costing him plenty. Unlike Uncertain Merton, John tends to be self-effacing, hides inside a shell.

You can get him to speak for himself by steps like these:

1. *Tell him why you want his opinions.* "It's important for me to get *everyone's* views, John. That's the only way I can get a complete picture."

2. *Coax him along.* Frequently, he holds back because he's not sure of himself. Good antidote is to start by asking him questions *to which he's likely to know the answer.* Note his relative strengths and weaknesses in these areas:

. . . *facts.* Giving information about his work usually finds him on firmest ground.

. . . *opinion.* Making comments about other people's ideas for work situations is next easiest for him.

. . . *ideas.* Here's where he needs most encouragement. Show him you like people who voice their views—gripes or otherwise; that you applaud suggestions even if they don't pan out.

3. *Praise his successes.* When he finally starts coming out of his shell, speaks up, makes a contribution on his own, make your approval crystal clear: "John, that was a great idea . . ."

▶ RECAP ◀

To clinch your approach to problem people, remember these high-lights:

The tool: the array of steps you can take in coping with the thorn-in-the-side individual.

When to use it: when you're responsible for the person, as a super-visor, parent, or official of the group involved, and when the person turns out to be a problem child because he or she passes the three-point test:

He causes loss or damage.

The loss or damage persists.

There's no simple solution.

How to sharpen your problem child handling:

Apply these steps in your considerations:

1. Weigh the gains and losses.

2. Ask yourself, "What can be changed?"

3. Don't make his problem your problem.

4. Tell him the truth about his position.

Finally, use the problem children covered at the end of the chapter as examples of how to proceed in specific cases.

chapter 14

In October, 1963, one of the most astonishing developments of all time rocked the sports world. To everyone's amazement and against the predictions of all the experts, Walter Alston's Dodgers pulled off a stunning four-game sweep against the famous and favored New York Yankees in the World Series. Pitcher Sandy Koufax emerged as the hero of the Series, credited with wins in two out of the four games.

How did Manager Walter Alston regard the victory? "Sure, Sandy was great," he said of his pitcher, "but it was *teamwork* that won the Series."

We Americans have a natural inclination towards teamwork. Our most popular sports —baseball, basketball, football —all require team play. And it's this inclination towards team play that sparks every aspect of our national life, and of our national accomplishment.

Learn *now* how to create this spirit among the people you work with, and you can

create team spirit — and convert a group into a powerful team

transfer the great benefits of teamwork to every enterprise in which you're involved in business or at home.

The business world increasingly has become an arena in which team activities rule the day. Go back some 75 years and you'll find a different state of affairs. The business world used to be dominated by loners, individual entrepreneurs who dominated banking, mining, chemicals, and other industries. The Morgans, Du Ponts, Rockefellers, Astors—their names stand as monuments to an era of individual enterprise.

Progress and invention were largely the result of individual effort and genius. Edison, Bell, Steinmetz—the pages of technological progress are lighted by individual genius.

With the turn of the century, however, came a change that has accelerated more and more. The fact is, problems have become too vast for individual capability. Competition and opportunity called for group effort, *team play*.

Dause L. Bibby of Remington Rand states the case for teamwork this way: "The day of one-man intuitive rule is dead. No one man, whatever his talents and dedication, can be expected to know all the facts about all facets of his organization. New technologies, customer demands, increasing competition and marketing research combined to produce one awesome fact: We have more information than we know how to use. Within this changed climate we at Remington Rand initiated a team approach to translate ideas into profitable products."

Earle Langeland, president of American Maize-Products Company, Roby, Indiana, makes a comment and provides a specific example:

"The small team has been our mainstay in cases needing quick, sustained attention. Recently as the price-cost squeeze on profits became acute, a group consisting of production manager, engineering manager, plant controller and a special projects man, came up with a 35-point profit improvement plan in a little over a week's time."

Note, from Langeland's example, how the small team substitutes for the one-man effort under today's high-pressure conditions.

How do you marry minds?

Since group action must play a major part in business and community activities today, the individual who knows how to marry minds—to create teams that function effectively—is clearly the one who'll make the highest score.

However, building a team requires more than simply getting a group together, giving them assignments and then sitting back and waiting for results. Casey Stengel, one of the foxiest managers in the business, discovered the failure of that approach as his New York Mets set an all-time record for *lack* of accomplishment in the '63 baseball season.

The French have a word for it

How do you convert a group of people from a loose disjointed assemblage into a smooth-running powerful unit? How do you get them all pulling in the same direction instead of against each other? How do you imbue them with the will to "go out there and fight"?

The French have a phrase, *esprit de corps* that tags the magic ingredient. The term "team spirit" is a good enough translation to set up the problem for us. The problem of teamwork in *non-sport* areas is actually a lot tougher than in sports like baseball, football, basketball, soccer, hockey and so on.

In sports there is a tradition that works *in favor* of teamwork. Kids absorb it in pickup ball games in the corner lot or in the park. That's why, if you want to see teamwork in action, watch a Little League game, or a high school contest.

In the kind of teamwork that is more common for us—that required in business or in community programs—there are fewer guidelines. Let's say you're in charge of fund-raising for your church or your club. You have six volunteers, all eager to do a job. You're handicapped, however. You don't have the same ready-made situation that favors the baseball manager.

In your case, the situation is what psychologists describe as "unstructured." You pretty much have to tell the individuals the roles they will have to assume, help them develop an approach in their activity and so on.

Let's get back to the heart of the problem, *esprit de corps*. How do we create that essential element that makes a team play way over its head and accomplish real miracles?

There are specific steps that you can take to build a surging, effective team. Each, by itself, is simple, obvious. Taken together, they help you forge an astonishing source of power and effectiveness that will prove once again that "the whole is greater than the sum of its parts."

A key secret of teamwork

Business executives—*notably those in companies that don't know how to build teamwork*—worry about morale. Psychologists who have studied the problem have come up with an answer:

"The employees are alienated from their work. They see no connection between what they are doing and the over-all goals of their organization."

I. Tell them the purpose

Every group, every organization, every business has a purpose. If it didn't have one, it wouldn't exist. A business firm may manufacture steel girders or paper cups, airplanes or pins. It may be a distributor of autos or a department store, a hotel or a laundry. But whether it is a manufacturer, distributor or service, it is meeting the wants of a community.

Connected with this business purpose is the objective of bringing in profits that can assure continued employment, wages and salaries to the employees and dividends to the stockholder. Whatever the purpose or objective of your group may be, *you use it to cement your team.*

Executives will tell you that office workers frequently have only the vaguest idea of how what they're doing connects with the firm's over-all objectives. For example:

Mimi Jenkins, a typist in the Acme Artisian Company, makes a mistake in the order she sends to the shipping department. She types part No. 3 instead of No. 13 and the wrong shipment goes out. On a farm somewhere a family will be without its water supply another week or so.

Would Mimi have been as likely to make that mistake if she had seen herself as part of a supply line bringing water to the thirsty? To see that, she must be told the purpose of her typing, the relation of her job to the shipping department where she works, the purpose of her company and its product.

Consider the great work done by our Peace Corps. Interviews with many of the Peace Corps workers turn up the same information. They are dedicated, effective workers because *they know the purpose of their team, the organization they serve.* They are fully aware that by transmitting American know-how to underdeveloped countries, they are performing a double duty: improving the lot of the underprivileged and at the same time spreading the American message of political and economic enlightenment. Does it help them work better? Yes. More effectively? Yes. Accomplish more? No question about it.

To tell others the purpose of the group or team means you must first know it yourself. Usually, the founders of organizations in their wisdom develop a statement of purpose.

There is no simple way to measure it, of course, but there's no question that one of the keystones of America's greatness lies in its statement of purpose, the Declaration of Independence. You remember:

> When in the Course of human events it becomes necessary for one people to dissolve the political bands which have connected them with another . . . a decent respect to the opinions of mankind requires that they should declare the causes which impel them to the separation. We hold these truths to be self-evident, that all men are created equal, that they are endowed by their Creator with certain unalienable rights, that among these are Life, Liberty and the Pursuit of Happiness.

How often, how many hundreds of thousands of people not only in America, but throughout the world have been uplifted in heart and mind and galvanized into high-minded action by this glorious statement of national purpose?

If you're in doubt about the purpose of the team you're heading up or trying to organize, think it through, take the time to put it down in black and white. Here are some examples:

An *historical society*. "Our purpose is to preserve the valuable homes and buildings, objects and traditions of the past to insure the pride of succeeding generations in our inheritance."

When new members join the society, the best way to get them "on the team" is to acquaint them with the organization's objectives.

A *football team*. "Fellows," says the coach in the Knute Rockne tradition, "you're here for just one reason—to win this game!"

An *annual party committee of almost any organization*. "Ladies and gentlemen, we want to set ourselves just one objective: to make this year's affair one of the most interesting and successful anniversary parties we've ever had."

If you're in doubt about the purpose of the group, check around with others, get their views or knowledge.

"Gene," says one puzzled leader, "I know I'm in charge of the membership committee, but exactly what is the committee supposed to do?"

The answer may be, welcome new members that appear or organize a drive for new members. Whatever it is, the leader must be perfectly clear on it, to be able to pass it along to team members.

Usually, the objective of a group requires action: there's something to be accomplished. You multiply the effectiveness of telling your group the purpose when you are specific:

"We want to raise $5,000 . . ."

"We want to attract 50 new members . . ."

"We want every single adult in the community to know what the school bond issue is about . . ."

In addition to the *what*, pin down the *when*. Set a time goal, or deadline:

"We must reach our quota by July 1st."

"We have until next week to cover the area."

"By the end of the year, we must show definite results—100% improvement . . ."

Once you've told the group the purpose or goal you're ready for the next step. What the next step is becomes clear when we examine an outstanding example of teamwork that took place in World War II:

On many of our larger warships, a deck officer was stationed with a microphone giving a play-by-play description of the battle over the ship's communications system. When a Kamikaze went down off the bow, every seaman on the ship knew of it immediately. That kept every man on the team united through the most critical hours.

This example of the Navy's successful effort to build teamwork gives us a clue to the second rule of building an effective team:

2. Tell them the score

People have to know more than the goal; they must know where they stand in relation to it. Sailors in a lifeboat will pull harder on the oars if they know they're headed in the right direction. The Naval officer at the microphone describes the battle for the men below decks because they must know the score if they're to throw their full weight behind the team.

That's why progress reports are so important: "Only 100 more envelopes to address and we're finished," says the woman in charge of getting out a club mailing. And her "team" redoubles its efforts.

Progress reports don't have to be formal, but they *do* have to be informative.

They don't have to be detailed, but they *should* show a sense of direction.

They don't have to come at regular intervals, but they *should* be frequent enough to remind your people of the purpose and where the team stands in relation to it.

In some cases, progress can be reported in sharp, unmistakable terms. This is true when your goal can be stated in numbers. For example, the supervisor of a molding shop can say, "At our present rate, we will produce 10% above quota by the end of the month."

Some other ways in which the "score" may be stated:

The workers of an office supply company would get some feeling of accomplishment if they could be told, "The memos on the desk of the President of the United States of America are held together by our clips."

The American businessman has become particularly adept in keeping track of progress. One example: The chart in the office of the sales executive that shows him weekly sales of his field staff.

The president of a service organization devoted to the placement of "office temporaries" has his own way of keeping his finger on the pulse of progress. In his office is a map with green tacks in every locality his firm serves. His weekly newsletter to his "team" reads, "Last week we opened our 27th office in Dallas, Texas!"

"Coach," says the tensed-up, raring-to-go quarterback, "if you don't put me out there on the field before the game's over, I'm just going to blow up and vanish in a cloud of smoke."

The moral? Building team spirit creates a kind of benign cycle. Once you generate team spirit in a team member, you have to provide an outlet. Accordingly, the third step is:

3. Help them make their contribution

The example of the quarterback makes it clear that you must provide the opportunity for team members to use the steam that you've helped create. Obviously, you want their contribution to be as constructive as possible, and *for* the team.

In getting them to make their contribution to team accomplishment, keep these things in mind:

. . . *proper placement.* Put each team member in the spot he'll be able to fill most effectively. On the work scene, this matter of proper assignment has been developed to a fine art. Personnel directors, for example, have become keenly aware that a girl who has what it takes to be an excellent receptionist may flop as a file clerk, and vice versa.

In other words, *assign your people to the team position they are best qualified to fill.*

. . . help them function effectively. It's up to the leader or the supervisor of the team to keep things clicking. This is largely a matter of seeing that everyone on the team carries out his assignment.

That's why the successful coach is in there every minute, keeping tabs on each player. That's why the effective supervisor makes his daily rounds checking each member of his team. If help is needed, he tries to provide it. As problems arise, he gets into a huddle with whoever is stymied.

"What's your opinion of your boss?"

Employees have frequently been surveyed regarding their opinions of their superiors. One of the most frequent and damaging complaints that turns up:

"My boss never gives me credit for what I do.

"If things go wrong, he takes it out on us. If things go right, he takes all the credit for himself."

This survey finding cues us in our next rule for building teamwork:

4. Let them know their personal contribution

Being part of a team is a good feeling. But a person wants to know where he stands in relation to the team, wants to feel that he's of value to it.

Team words

First of all, you want to keep reminding a team member that he's on the team. Here, the very words you use can work wonders. Whether you're talking to individual members or the group as a whole, use *team words*—words like *we, us, our.*

Your language should always be slanted to suggest the idea that, "*Our* success depends on *you.*"

Don't let anyone forget they belong to the team. Bring the sensitive or timid person into your group discussions. Ask him questions you know he can answer. Ask him for ideas, always indicating that he is contributing to the whole group in giving them: "Hank, can you give us an idea on this problem?"

Even if Hank may not be able to produce an idea on the spur of the moment, you've given him one—that he's a respected member of the team.

Pin medals—and make a daydream come true

One of our pleasantest daydreams finds us in the spotlight for some praiseworthy feat, while the applause of the multitude thunders in our ears.

When a team member does a good job, he wants appreciation. He deserves it. You give him his reward by coming as close as you can to bringing our common daydream to reality. Your public praise and expressions of approval for outstanding work further cement the team.

One problem may arise: the green-eyed monster may threaten the stability of the team. Be sure to handle occasions of commendation so as to avoid any resentment or envy on the part of the others. You do this, for example, when you get in a word of appreciation for those who helped. For example:

Ed Lane, sales manager for a company that makes and sells work-shoes, tells the man who landed a big hunting-boot order: "That was a beautiful job of striking while the iron's hot, Fred, and you've got a lot of credit coming. And how about that cooperation you got from the Order Department and Shipping . . ."

Word your praise so that the team idea comes through. Treat the man's individual success in terms of its contribution to the group. As one committee chairman said: "Jim's telephone campaign put us ahead of every other group in the organization."

Notice that little word with the big effect—us.

Problem: build a "perfect" team

The four steps above show you how to build team spirit, how to get people to do their best and pull together for the team's sake.

From time to time you may be faced with a special problem in the team area: you may be asked to line up a team from scratch, put together a group of people to accomplish a given objective, say, the one of developing a profit improvement plan like that described by Earle Langeland of American Maize-Products.

When you're given the job of creating a team—it may be a committee or a task force on the job or off—you may find yourself stopped cold by a basic problem: Who should you put on the team? What combination of people will work out best? Who will be able to contribute the most to achieving group goals?

What to look for

To some extent, the answer depends on what the team is supposed to accomplish. Different tasks impose different team requirements. A group that will deliver top results in organizing a picnic may be incapable of developing a set of by-laws for an organization.

A team with an informational objective must be able to gather data, to probe and analyze and to come up with conclusions based on the findings. On the other hand, a group with the goal of organizing a publicity campaign or safety drive must be able to plan, recruit people, prepare educational material, explain instructions, and so on.

The six basic qualities

The interesting fact is, there is a specific answer for the problem of building the ideal team. Here it is:

Your team is likely to be most effective if its members possess six key characteristics. These six characteristics may be found in one, two or three individuals. In some cases, they may be spread over a larger number. If you're ever handed the problem of organizing a team, make sure these types are represented, and your team is sure to be a winner:

The dynamo. He's the pusher, the nudger, the one who's aware of deadbeats and deadlines.

The hard-head. He's the man who says, "I know it's never been done this way before. Let's try it." He helps keep the group's feet on the ground. He's apt to be called a realist or a cynic.

The analyst. He's outstandingly cerebral, he uses his brain the way others use their fists. While others may gloat over how well things are going, he's worrying about tomorrow. He's a sharp trouble-spotter.

The artist. His specialty is creative thinking. He'll produce ten suggestions while others are laboring to come up with one. He often needs to be controlled. Someone—usually the hard-head—must separate the wheat from the chaff of his mental output. But the artist is essential if the task requires something new and different.

Smith College Professor Michael S. Olmsted, in his book, *The Small Group*, has this to say of the "artist":

"In actual groups, one often encounters a member with a flow of original ideas and another member who, though he has no particular ideas of his own, is adept at putting together the contribution of others . . . they are different functions."

The detail man. He has a head for figures and the patience to stick with them. He'll take pains, split hairs, double and triple check. For complicated tasks, where many small elements must be integrated, he can be a life-saver.

The team player. His outstanding quality is loyalty to the cause. You can wake him at two in the morning and ask him to hop a plane to Tokyo, and he'll go without a grumble.

A case history

In practice, there tends to be a strong connection between the function of the team member and the quality he brings to the effort. A case history described by John H. Kostmayer, vice-president at First Investors Corporation, sponsor and distributor of mutual fund plans, makes this relationship clear:

"We had the problem of creating a new visual presentation. We appointed a group consisting of a sales manager as leader, the training coordinator, a writer, an artist and an expert in regulatory matters. The leader was given wide latitude and was made responsible for keeping me posted on progress, probable costs, and regulatory considerations.

"The group functioned successfully. The leader provided the necessary impetus; the creative personnel were prolific in their production of ideas; the training consultant saw to it that the presentation remained teachable and learnable; our expert on regulatory affairs saw to it that we complied in detail with the necessary regulations."

Why teams work

One of the reasons given by psychologists to explain the effectiveness of team effort is that members get a sense of reinforcement, that they are stimulated by the feeling that they are part of something bigger than themselves.

Accordingly, you'll find two reactions among team members:

. . . they like to be reminded that they're not alone in their efforts, that if they need help the team is there to give it to them.

. . . by working on a team, by being part of a larger group, they can achieve goals that would be far beyond their reach if they were alone.

Literature provides one of the greatest examples of a team in which each member was for the team, and the team was devoted to each member. The team? You find it described in "The Three Musketeers," by Alexandre Dumas. And their motto tells a great deal about the spirit of the successful team: "All for one and one for all!"

Find the occasion and the words to tell this to your people, and you'll have a winning team every time.

▶ Recap ◀

To become the master coach, the outstanding team leader, remember that we live in an age where the lone genius has given way to the power-packed team.

You build team spirit by taking these steps:
1. Tell them the purpose
2. Tell them the score
3. Help them make their contribution
4. Let them know their personal contribution

Then, to form a "perfect" team, find people like these to put on it:

The dynamo
The hard-head
The analyst
The artist
The detail man
The team player

Finally, remind people that it's "all for one and one for all," use team words like *we, us, our*—and you've got it made.

chapter 15

"Women!"

How many men in how many different situations have cried out in anger and frustration at the so-called fair sex? The mystery of women is as old as the race; the problem of dealing with them started with Eve.

The Book of Proverbs in the Old Testament underlines the unpredictability of affairs involving women. The ancient prophet says: "There be three things which are too wonderful for me, yea, four which I know not: The way of an eagle in the air; the way of a serpent upon a rock; the way of a ship in the midst of the sea; and the way of a man with a maid."

Of course, we know dealing with women is a problem in other than the romantic sphere. This chapter will largely concentrate on dealing with women on the work scene. As appropriate, however, case histories involving problems off the work scene will also appear.

how to
handle women
— strengthening
your hold
on the
weaker sex

Many an unfortunate male has gotten his comeuppance not only because he was at a disadvantage in dealing with the opposite sex, but in mistakenly thinking that he knew how. For instance:

Frank Chapin of Portland, Maine, was put in charge of an assembly department with both male and female employees. His boss told him, "Frank, I know you'll do fine, dealing with the men. What about the women?"

"No problem," said Frank confidently. "The way I see it, women are just little men."

In two weeks, Frank had to be yanked out of the assembly job and given an assignment where he headed an all male unit.

To what extent was his view that "women are just little men" to blame for his downfall? It would be difficult to say. But even if this idea were at the bottom of his trouble, he shouldn't be criticized too strongly. The fact is, during World War II, when many women went to work for the first time, a group of learned "experts" put out a pamphlet on the female employee. "Treat women," advised this booklet, "just as though they were little men."

This statement, as Frank's experience suggests, contains as much useful wisdom as the idea that, "Men are big women!"

Women are different!

The last source from which you would expect a statement on the nature of women would probably be the *Wall Street Journal*. Yet this staid business publication on November 6, 1963, carried an editorial:

"Mere males must approach the subject (of women) with trepidation and maybe smart ones wouldn't at all . . . It seems rather obvious that since only women can be wives and mothers, the role of women in society is bound to be different from that of men."

And the editorial adds some statistics that remind us of the increasing importance of women on the work scene (her importance at home is traditional):

"The huge influx of women into the labor force is one of the most striking parts of the employment picture in recent years. Not only that: the number of working wives is sharply rising. Today, about one-third of America's 40 million married women are in the labor force against about a quarter only a decade ago."

"You can't live with them and you can't live without them," goes the old saying about the fair sex. This chapter will avoid the personal problem aspects of women: their social role, marital relations, etc. However, it's obvious that any book that presumes to talk about the mastery and management of people cannot logically ignore half the human race. Accordingly, we will try to be constructive without being chauvinistic, specific without being impertinent, helpful without being patronizing.

This chapter will hew to four specifics:

- The *basic differences* that distinguish women from men.
- How *different types of women* react in their relationships.
- How you tackle *problem situations* in which women tend to become involved.
- How to deal with a special but particularly difficult and tantalizing problem: that of *the beautiful female in the workgroup.*

And finally, a brief quiz will give you the chance to learn the answer to an intriguing question: How well do you know women?

Physical differences

The physical differences that distinguish women from men are supposedly those that prompted the storied Frenchman to cry, "*Vive la différence!*"

Tests have been made to ascertain the actual nature of variances between male and female. Here are the facts:

The average woman's physical strength is about half the average man's. Even a large woman will not be as powerful as a small man. Her muscles are long and slim, while a man's muscles are made for heavier work.

Women's bone structure is such that her greatest strength is in the thigh and pelvic regions, to help her carry out the process of bearing children. Her internal structure on the whole is unsuitable for long periods of standing. She can't take unbroken pressure or long periods of unbroken activity. On the other hand, she's less susceptible to cold and heat.

The recent feat of the first Russian girl astronaut, Valentina Tereshkova, proves that the fair sex has the physical stamina needed to pioneer in outer space along with her male opposite number.

Where women score high

You don't have to be a biologist to know that women are different from men. A single glance tells you. However, psychologists using aptitude tests have probed deeper than the eye can see. They discovered that there are specific skills in which women excel:

. . . *speed of hand and finger operations.* Accordingly, women are superior for such jobs as small parts assembly, typing, and for work requiring the use of small precision tools.

. . . *better sight and color sense.* Actually, the ratio of color blindness as between men and women is 8 to 1. Women excelled in all tests that involved matching off or pairing items by shape or color.

. . . *patience.* Women adjust to routine work much better than men. The average woman is superior to the average man in doing exacting work. She pays more attention to details.

Their unique attitudes

In their values and judgments, women may differ markedly from men:

. . . that's why there's a "women's vote." Women are influenced by a candidate's appearance.

. . . women tend to "take things personally." One psychologist illustrates it by this example: Ask a man, "Where did you buy this steak?" He'll answer: "At Doyle's market." Ask his wife the same question, and she'll answer with some emotion: "Why? What's wrong with it?"

Translated the implication here is that a *woman tends to see almost everything in terms of herself.*

The next point is closely related to the one just covered:

. . . women tend to become emotional. An offhand comment, even the slightest bit critical, may bring on a storm of tears. The reason is, when you discuss her work, a woman is likely to think you're discussing *her.* That's why it's even more important in dealing with women than with men to follow the rules of criticism: link criticism with encouragement and appreciation; be quicker to praise outstanding performance in women.

. . . their feelings tend to focus on people. A man may be loyal to an ideal, an organization. A woman will be loyal to her boss, the president or head of an organization.

The next point is an extension of the previous one:

. . . women are more interested in people than in things. For example, talk to a woman about her work, and unlike a man who will describe machines and methods, she will tell you about her co-workers, boss, and so on.

Most women who work can give you more information about others in their departments than any personnel file could hold.

. . . women have to talk. The kaffeeklatsch is undoubtedly a female invention. Is this love of chitchat undesirable? Not necessarily.

Three researchers at Harvard University reported their findings in a study of one company situation:

"The only way the women felt they could make their work-life interesting and meaningful was through conversation with one another, and the development of informal groups."

Should you try to stop their talk in the interest of getting work done? Heavens, no! You can use this fact in your favor. As the head of a radio assembly department says:

"The work in my department is monotonous. I know it, so does everybody else. But my girls perform to a high standard because I let them chat while they work. Since the operation is routine, they can do it while talking to their neighbors. And it's the talk that makes the work easy for them."

. . . they tend to conform. You may ask, "Don't men?" Yes, but not to the same extent.

Remember the "new look" in women's clothes? It was bitterly resented by millions of women—but they all finally succumbed and let their hems down.

However, don't be mousetrapped into telling any individual female she's "typical." Conform as they may, they still want to be considered "special." Watch a veteran dress salesman or hairdresser's approach. You get the idea fast that the customer he happens to be talking to is the only one he's *really* interested in.

Water the idea down, use it sincerely by showing the women you deal with that each *is* special, and you'll get any reasonable result you seek.

. . . women use indirection. They won't always come right out and say what they mean—and thereby get their reputation for cattiness:

"Helen never looked better," one tells another. Translation: "Helen, poor girl, looks as terrible as usual."

Or: Bill Jones, walking to church with his wife on a summer Sunday, hears: "See how well Charlie Wilson looks in his new straw hat!" Translation: "Bill, you need a new hat."

The foregoing paragraphs remind us that women require special attention and treatment. The facts given can't guarantee to keep you out of trouble. Even 1000 pages of facts wouldn't be enough to do that. However, the pointers given here will improve a hundredfold your chances of staying clear of the quicksand that women, intentionally or otherwise, sometimes create. And furthermore, you'll be prepared to develop pleasant and constructive relationships, help women themselves be happier and more effective. So now we turn to:

Some female types—and how to handle them

There are as many different types of women as there are types of men. The most that can be said is that a given woman falls into a general classification only in the roughest sense.

But broad generalizations can be useful as *general* guides, always remembering the differences in degree. Let's look at several types from the standpoint of a colleague or possibly a boss who might have to deal with them in a job situation:

1. *The career woman.* She wants to get ahead on her own. She feels she can handle her job as well or better than any man. She won't thank you for any statement or implication to the contrary.

As a matter of fact, she has a keen competitive streak which becomes exaggerated when her competitor is a man. Marriage doesn't interest her too much. The job comes first.

Biggest danger in handling her: That you might patronize her or treat her professional pretensions slightingly.

Most important measures in dealing with her: Treat her with the same respect as you would anyone else in her position. On the other hand, don't be deceived by her show of hard-headedness and independence. She is as eager as anyone for friendliness and open communication.

2. *The old maid*. Not every unmarried woman falls into this category, but there is a type who takes on the pattern naturally.

The difference between her and the career woman is that the old maid would *prefer* marriage to work. Unhappily, her knight on a white horse just hasn't shown up. In the absence of a family she probably wants, this woman compensates by making her job a substitute for many other things. Her work is likely to be paramount and she usually is a loyal employee.

Biggest danger in handling her: She may irritate other women who are not so completely concentrated on their work as she is.

Most important measures in dealing with her: Let her know that you're aware of her helpfulness to others, when that's the case. However, if she's really annoying others, call her attention to it gently at first, more firmly if the situation continues.

You can expect steady performance over long periods of time. However, don't be surprised by sudden fits of depression during which the quality of her work slips. Avoid criticism at this time, look for ways to ease her burden and point out her accomplishments. Otherwise it may take her longer to bounce back.

3. *The married woman*. This type on the job is usually a mature person with a real sense of responsibility.

Biggest danger in handling her: As she is holding down *two* jobs—at home and at work—she has her own particular problems. You have to keep these in mind, even make special exceptions to help her cope with her special variety of moonlighting.

Most important measures in dealing with her:

Try to use her maturity to advance group goals. Encourage her to come up with suggestions. As a married woman with a household to run, she is likely to be an efficient "management engineer." Her experience can pay off with good ideas.

4. *The would-like-to-be-married woman*. She's waiting for knight to fall. She's marking time, not really interested in anything but snaring a man. In the future, she may join the old maid ranks, but her youth makes her a different problem.

Because of her preoccupation, she has few incentives to work really hard. She'd trade in her company badge for wedding bells in one second flat. And this poses a work problem.

Biggest danger in handling her: That her superior gives up trying to get her perform up to par, accepting the idea that "she won't be around very long, anyhow." However, if she's given this license to drift, others will want the same privilege. You can't blame them. And if her boss tries to justify her foot-dragging, and demands full performance from everybody else, the fight's on.

Most important measures in dealing with her:

1. Give her a sense of purpose on the job by showing her how her work affects others: fellow employees, customers, the company itself.

2. Appeal to her self-esteem: "Mary, you don't want to leave a record of failure behind you."

3. Use the "no exception" principle: One executive who's experienced with this type of girl tells her: "You may only work here another month or week. But even if it's for a single day, I expect you to do the job, just as everybody else does." It works.

Typical problems women can be at the bottom of

Females can cause thorny problems that make the witches' scene from *Macbeth* seem like a taffy pull. It's not necessarily because they're mean and nasty. It's more an outgrowth of woman's role in our society. Attribute it to biology, or the stars. The point is, women tend to create problems of a particular pattern. Here are some of the kinds of situations involving women that have bewildered their bosses:

The Triangle. Much to his surprise, a male boss has sometimes found himself caught in the crossfire of two women, each vying for his attention or favor. The situation may have no romantic angle whatsoever. What are the women fighting for? An unofficial position that may be described as "the favorite."

If you're unlucky enough to be the object of such a duel—

. . . make sure you *don't* play favorites. The woman who loses will be a constant source of trouble to you—and so will the one who wins.

. . . watch out for their approaches. Women who want to show they've got "more of an in" with the boss than anyone else will push their attempts subtly: "When the new typewriter comes in, Mr. Doe, I hope you give it to me. My machine has been on its last legs for months."

Sound like a logical request? Yes, it does. But actually, it may be a request for something that is actually an undeserved privilege. And if the girl gets her way—and particularly if she *doesn't* deserve it—she'll use the incident to "prove" she's Number One in the office.

. . . if the situation seems to be getting out of hand, take up the matter in private with the more aggressive of the two women. This calls for maximum tact. Don't indulge in personalities. Keep your talk general: "Harriet, I've been concerned lately with the morale in the office. I feel that, for one reason or another, tensions have been unnecessarily created. Do you have any ideas on the subject?" If you keep tossing the ball to her, she'll get the import of your words, will respect you for your diplomacy, and in most cases, will defer to your implied request for harmony.

The waterfountain romance. Cupid can cause as much havoc on the work scene as the god of war.

The manager of an extrusion department in a plastics plant put the problem this way:

"Love may be pink clouds for the principals, but for others it may trigger the blackest feelings. Envy, jealousy, a dozen destructive reactions can result from romance on the job."

Of course, the comment above doesn't reflect the many cases that are healthy, discreet, and may even lead to marriage. "Normal" romantic attachments between employees in the same company or department rarely come to general attention. They are carried on after office hours and off the premises.

However, if a raging, all-too-evident romance is causing actual interference with the work, take these steps—cautiously, and certain that you have *reason* to act:

. . . let the man involved know that you have become aware of what's going on because efficiency is suffering.

. . . keep the conversation businesslike. "John, this isn't a personal matter, as far as I'm concerned. My interest is in maintaining the efficiency and decorum of the office . . ." If you smell trouble in the situation because a married person is involved, bring up anonymous examples from the past to show why it has to stop.

. . . use the "people are beginning to notice" approach to explain your action.

. . . ask that the situation be straightened out or kept outside company premises.

And, as a final step, you might have to warn the man in the case that if he can't solve the problem, somebody may have to be transferred or discharged.

Under no circumstances do you want to butt into the private affairs of your people. You're neither a censor nor a wet blanket. For this reason, the primary rule is that you make no move *unless* there is interference with the work or well-being of the department.

The rain-of-tears attack. The one tendency of women that unnerves most men is their proneness to tears. It may come without warning. And it's devastating to the ordinary male, especially when he can't figure out what started it. For example:

A puzzled father finds his teen-age daughter, head down, raining tears on her history book.

"What's wrong, Honey?"

"I don't know."

"Well, there must be a reason."

"I must see 'Lawrence of Arabia' again. I don't know, I think I'm in love with Lawrence, or Peter O'Toole (the actor playing the part of Lawrence) or something, but I've just got to see that picture again . . ."

The wise father here will simply accept the ways of love, comfort the girl, and possibly arrange to take her to see the movie that stars the man she adores. However, when you're dealing with an adult, and the cause of the woman's tears are beyond your personal control, here's the most you can do:

. . . let her recover her self-control. Don't dismiss a tearful girl with an off-hand: "Go wash your face, you'll feel better." She may, but she won't feel better toward you for dismissing her feelings so lightly.

. . . let her know you're available to discuss anything she wants to bring up, but *don't pry.*

. . . if you're involved in her outburst, if you've brought on the tears by thoughtless criticism, for example, explain the situation, kindly and in detail. Show her you want her to understand why you said or did what you did.

You don't want to be harsh, but keep in mind that some women use tears as a deliberate weapon. Whatever happens, you have to maintain your standards—undiluted by the tears.

And now, one of the toughest situations in the entire male-female confrontation is that of a girl whose natural charms are so plentiful that she tends to cause an emotional tornado in an otherwise peaceful landscape. We're talking about:

The beautiful-girl problem

There's one aspect of the woman-at-work problem that is as intriguing as it is disturbing, as provocative as it is bewildering. Every supervisor who has had a problem with this type of female has never forgotten it. Every writer in the human relations field has tackled the problem.

The editors of the trade journal, *Chemical Engineering*, discovered that this type of woman problem tends to crop up frequently in companies that operate in advanced technological areas. For this reason, *Chemical Engineering* ran an article that proved to be tremendously popular with its readers, entitled: "Beauty and the Boss." As seasoned executives will tell you, female pulchritude perils any work scene.

The too-beautiful employee. Helen of Troy is the prototype. She launched a thousand ships, all right, and plenty of men got killed when the ships got going.

Latter-day Helens turn up on the job, women whose good looks might be great on a magazine cover, but cause havoc on the job.

A *Girl of Disturbing Beauty.* "Pardon me if I seem to be upset," said Manager Pete Jansen, "but I am."

The personnel executive nodded. "What's on your mind?"

"I'd like you to transfer the secretary you hired two weeks ago."

A disbelieving smile touched the older man's lips. "You mean that beautiful girl . . ."

The project head nodded.

"But her tests were excellent."

"She's a bright girl. I have no complaint on that score."

"Then what's wrong?"

The engineer hesitated. "May I be perfectly frank, Mr. Fleming? Having her around interferes with my work. I'll be much better off with a plain Jane who shows a pulchritude index down around zero."

"Monstrous," you may say on reading the above. "Lives there a man with soul so dead that he can't take one of nature's wonders in stride? Now if I were in Pete Jansen's shoes . . ."

"Yes," most of us would say, "if I had to pick a problem, having a beautiful secretary is the one I'd choose." Beauty, lush female beauty, promises to be desirable adornment for any man's office. If the paneling is mahogany, a blonde is perfect. If the paneling is blonde, a brunette charmer adds just the right note.

Chances are you'd be making a serious mistake. Ordinarily we don't think of female pulchritude as a liability. But many women before and since Helen of Troy have triggered trouble. The fact is, on the work scene, beauty can be beastly.

Venus as trouble maker

A United Press dispatch datelined Manila starts off: "The 300 women employees of the government service insurance system were warned today against love on the company premises."

Manager Rodolfo P. Andal, in an effort to keep the romance angle under control, set up a special ruling for the beauties in the department. He specifically prohibited "overtime for attractive female employees."

Beauty, they say, is skin deep. But that's deep enough to cause plenty of trouble. Entire departments have been disrupted by a human Venus-at-large. Understandably, girls who have physical charms are seldom loath to display them.

Eyes wander, minds wander, and the work just doesn't get done as the potential Casanovas on the male side of the roster fight to keep their minds on their work.

There's something about the mixture of love and business that makes it explosive. One aspect of the problem:

"It's expensive," explains an insurance company department head, "employees begin to act as though the office were a gossip factory."

Knowing what to do and what not to do to prevent the presence of an on-the-job beauty queen from converting a department into a romantic battleground is essential:

1. *Avoid the ridiculous.* Don't try to set matters aright by adopting arbitrary rules of the "boys can't talk to girls" variety.

In the case of the Manila insurance bureau, Mr. Andal, known as "father of the firm," might make stick such regulations as, "Extended conversations between married men and single girls are prohibited." But in the ordinary case, that kind of move is usually a prelude to more grief.

2. *The invisible barrier.* The experienced master of people builds into the working atmosphere a sense of propriety that makes overly free relations between the sexes clearly out of place. Although it's an intangible element, it has specific aspects. For example:

. . . Horseplay, teasing on a boy-girl basis is promptly curbed.

. . . If a girl must work overtime or come in on Saturday, she shares the work with another girl.

3. *Apply the rule of reason.* Try an appeal to common sense for the girl who's too popular for her own good. You can make it clear that your office is a public place. Conduct that might be perfectly proper at a summer resort or the beach isn't necessarily O.K. at a desk or counter.

Give venus a screen test

The girl whom nature has endowed with more than her fair share of attractive attributes poses problems that must be considered the moment she shows up on the doorstep in the guise of a job applicant.

Experienced personnel directors have had to consider this type of problem from the point of company welfare. As a department or unit head these same questions may rise to plague you:

. . . *do her good looks overqualify her for an ordinary job?* For the moment think of the physical enchantment that the heartbreaker brings as just another personal qualification, such as an ability to type or run an adding machine.

Just as you wouldn't want to waste the talents of an expert typist on a job requiring a minimum amount of typing time, would it make sense to put an extremely attractive girl on a job like filing? After all, her physical attractiveness might be put to much better use as a receptionist, sales girl or perhaps a fashion or photographer's model.

. . . *is her beauty apt to make her less permanent on the job?* Turnover is always a problem. One vice-president of personnel states positively: "Pretty girls are much better bets for early marriage. I try to avoid hiring them simply because in my experience they're apt to be around only half as long as the plain Janes."

Such sweeping generalizations, of course, don't apply to specific cases. Yet logic seems to be on the side of the personnel executive's observation.

Certainly the costliness of turnover—in terms of retraining, temporary dislocation, and so on—suggests that any quality creating temporariness should be avoided.

But, of course, it's both unfair and an affront to nature to write off the pulchritudinous female as nothing more than a peck of trouble. Many beautiful women are capable of so comporting themselves, and so affecting those about them, that only the desirable, constructive reactions to their good looks are stimulated. In such cases, their loveliness emits a kind of radiance that uplifts everyone about them. You don't have to worry about females of this type. They can take care of themselves, and anyone who comes within range of their brilliant, dizzying eyes.

The beauty who's a problem to herself

The untimely demise of glamorous movie star Marilyn Monroe emphasized a point of which psychologists have long been aware. The beautiful girl or woman herself often suffers from problems that originate from her over-bountiful gifts of nature.

In his book, "Paradoxes of Everyday Life," psychiatrist Milton R. Sapirstein writes: "Outstanding beauty, like outstanding gifts of any kind, tends to get in the way of normal emotional development."

Dr. Sapirstein goes on to explain that the modern Helen, ". . . is, in a sense, smitten by her own beauty and the phantasies it nourishes in her collide head-on with those it has awakened in the man. The outcome cannot be happy. It is sometimes disastrous."

Accordingly, the beautiful woman often has problems of emotional stability, and of relating to those about her. These problems stem from feelings that have developed early in her life. When these problems are aggravated by the problems her co-workers may have in accepting her matter-of-factly, the situation can become untenable.

If, for example, her female co-workers treat her with distrust or barely repressed envy, it's clear that she will have no easy time becoming a normal member of the group.

And if among the male contingent, emotions are stirred up, the workgroup may suffer from difficulties ranging from competitiveness for the girl's favors to open physical conflict, should the situation become sufficiently inflamed.

One executive who was interviewed on the problem of the pulchritudinous secretary said, "In my experience, attractive girls in an office stimulate morale and productivity on the part of the males."

It's important to keep this observation in mind in arriving at any logical point of view. Certainly the dictum, "Fire the little darlings" would seem a travesty not only aesthetically but also from the viewpoint of managerial fairness.

The most valid statement on the problem seems to have been made by a department head who admitted that over the years he had faced the gorgeous gal problem several times:

"I think the wisest approach is to consider a girl's beauty as a special attribute, like being seven feet tall. In jobs where the particular attribute promises to be a problem, the girl just simply shouldn't be placed. But if there's nothing about the job that suggests it couldn't be done by the attractive girl, provided she has all the other qualifications, I think she's a safe bet. But of course it's up to the manager to see that he doesn't let himself be influenced in his treatment of her. The rest of the group will be watching, and any favoritism is likely to bring trouble."

Women—true or false?

Want to try your hand at a fast quiz that can tell you how well you've got the fair sex sized up? Below you'll find a number of statements about women. Are they true, or false? Test yourself, see how you score in your woman wisdom.

The fact is, a lot of things said—and in some cases, whispered— about women, are false. And, of course, a lot of it is true. Can you distinguish hard fact from defensive male vanity? If you get all twelve answers correct, you know a lot more about women than most of us.

	T	F
1. Women are more diplomatic than men.	✓	
2. Women are worse drivers than men.		✓
3. Women basically make better scientists.		✓
4. Women have lower IQ's than men.		✓

	T	F
5. Female supervisors are underrated.	___	___
6. Ladies are less predictable than men.	___	___
7. Women are less shrewd than men when it comes to investments.	___	___
8. Women think more analytically than men.	___	___
9. Working conditions and companions are more important to women than men.	___	___
10. Women are less productive than men.	___	___
11. Women have better color vision than men.	___	___
12. Maleness and femaleness are mutually exclusive qualities.	___	___

To see how you made out, check your answers against the ones provided below.

The answers

1. *True.* Men say women are "two-faced" because they can greet someone they don't like with cordiality, even apparent affection. Consciously or otherwise, the ladies try to mask their true feelings to maintain an easy atmosphere.

2. *False.* At least, insurance companies, who ought to know, don't think so. The only discrimination between sexes in this area suggests that the male of the species is deemed a greater risk. Auto insurance rates in some regions are much higher when a male under 25 drives the family car than when a female takes the wheel.

3. *False.* Our colleges produce very few women who become intellectually excited by, or immersed in, scientific problems. Men are well ahead in interest and accomplishment in almost all scientific fields.

4. *False.* In the early years, the girls have an edge. The lads catch up, but studies show little difference that can be ascribed to gender. However, opportunity to exercise intelligence still favors the male sex.

5. *True.* There's a psychological disadvantage in the fact that everybody expects the supervisor to be a man. Yet recent surveys indicate that females can make just as good leaders as males.

6. *False.* They are harder to understand for a person keyed to a masculine world. But any experienced husband can tell you that predictability multiplies with each bit of understanding acquired.

7. *False.* Brokers say the ladies, once they get the hang of what they are doing, can spot a good investment faster than the males. By the way, 52.5% of the individual owners of stocks traded on the New York Stock Exchange are women.

8. *False.* There are many women who think analytically, and many men who don't, but consistent differences in the performance of the two sexes favor the males in this respect.

9. *True.* While neither sex is happy about poor working conditions and uncongenial colleagues, these elements are more significant to the female.

10. *False.* Latest studies of output per man-hour (or woman-hour, if you prefer) reveal that women workers in all age groups show greater productivity than men, except in the 55–64 bracket, among whom there's no difference, and under 25 where male output is slightly higher.

11. *True.* Some 7 or 8 % of males have major defects in color vision, while less than .5% of females are so afflicted. This may be part of the reason for the general impression that the ladies have better taste. So when the wife or girl friend says that tie doesn't go with that suit, listen, if only because the studies show she's more likely to be right.

12. *False.* Each human being, male or female, is composed of both male and female components, and the proportion of one to the other varies widely in each person.

▶ RECAP ◀

To refresh yourself on the subject of dealing with women, remember these chapter highlights:

Remember that women really are *different.* They're not like "little men" any more than men are "big women." Their differences are physical, mental, and emotional. They have unique attitudes:

. . . they're influenced by appearances, such as a man's looks.

. . . they tend to "take things personally."

. . . they tend to become emotional.

. . . their feelings tend to focus on people.

. . . women like to talk.

. . . they tend to conform, but don't tell any female she's "typical." Understandably, each one likes to think she's "special."

. . . women use indirection.

You can make headway with women by learning how to deal constructively with such types as:

1. The career woman
2. The old maid
3. The married woman
4. The would-like-to-be-married woman

Also watch out for the typical problems women can be at the bottom of:

  . . . the triangle
  . . . the waterfountain romance
  . . . the rain-of-tears attack

Not too typical a problem, but a humdinger when it comes along: learn the difficulties and the remedies of dealing with the latter-day Helen of Troy, the beautiful gal who's got too much on the ball for the peace of mind of others around her.

Finally, to find out in a couple of minutes how much you know about the fair sex, take the brief true-false quiz with which this chapter concludes.

chapter 16

"Why," you may ask, "use a word like *incitement* when most authorities prefer the traditional *motivation?* That's what you're going to be talking about, isn't it, the motivation of people?"

As for many things, the answer lies in the dictionary: "*motivate:* to provide with a motive"; "*incite:* to arouse to action; spur or urge on."

Notice how much more action-oriented is the word *incite.* It's because motivation suggests indirection and the slow fuse that *incitement,* with its greater immediacy, won out.

The important element of pace, speed, degree of commitment, is the key to *superior* results. You don't have to be content with getting a man to do a job at a get-by level. Learn—*here and now*—how to *incite,* to imbue people with eagerness, and the desire to achieve. Yes, this chapter will cover the subject of motivation. But it will describe the Techniques of Incitement, to

incitement
— how to
get people
to give
more than they
know they have

show you how to get people to give in a *big way*—both to their gain, and yours.

When a person lacks motivation, invisible psychic gears shift, and the individual, if he moves at all, is in slow gear.

During World War II, Gene Millard was in charge of a department that made plastic bomb parts. Labor was scarce, and Personnel really had to scrape the bottom of the barrel to keep operations going.

Oliver Daksen, fiftyish, was hired to run one of Millard's forming presses. Weeks after he started, Daksen was still operating at only slightly better than a beginner's pace.

To Millard's attempts to motivate him, the slow-speed artist simply shrugged and said: "That's the way I work." Millard finally got fed up. "Damn it, Ollie," he yelled, "don't you realize there's a war on? Those parts you're making are protecting our boys over there. They don't need 'em next week, they need them yesterday!"

Despite himself, Gene Millard had hit the hot button. He had said the one thing that was needed to galvanize the employee into action. "You mean these things are for the Army?" Ollie asked.

"Darned right they are."

By the end of the week, Ollie's foot-dragging had been replaced by a briskness that matched anyone else's in the department.

What had happened to Ollie? What had been added to his mental makeup that led to his improved performance? Answer: *incitement* had been added.

Ollie's case is not unusual. And it doesn't take a war or a sudden infusion of patriotism to get outstanding performance. It's been demonstrated again and again: a lackadaisical individual, successfully incited, will move like a ball of fire.

Incitement from the sidelines

There is a familiar activity that clearly spells out the importance of incitement. It tends to flourish especially on weekends, generally involves the younger and more active members of the female sex. We're talking about a phenomenon known to school athletic fields all over the country —*cheerleading.*

What is the purpose of the leaping, shouting teamwork of the cheerleading corps but to urge on the diamond and gridiron warriors to greater and greater effort? This is incitement of a special order. And we've all seen the miracles that can take place on the sports arena when, at the cheerleaders' behest, the crowd screams, "We want a touchdown!" and the football team delivers.

Our culture has other means and devices for motivating people. The military band puts an extra snap into the limbs of the most fatigued soldiers. Old Glory radiating its stars and stripes against the sky may impel citizens to give what Lincoln called "the last full measure of devotion"—and embrace death itself, for a cause.

Literature abounds with examples of people, pushed to extremes of action, when effectively incited. One classic example of extreme but undesirable action is the bloody road of deceit and murder on which Macbeth embarks, when lured by the ambition to becoming king. Aspiration, love of power, has always been a prime inciter.

A more praiseworthy instance tells of the ancient Greeks, Damon and Pythias, whose friendship was so great, that Damon pledged his life on Pythias' word to return to Syracuse by a certain time, while Pythias fought against tremendous odds to keep the date, even though his life would be forfeited if he arrived too late. Friendship can be one of the strongest forces for incitement that exists.

Incitement can influence men, nations—and young boys. Note what happens to young Johnny Fabre . . .

Wisdom in a woodpile

There are more commonplace examples of successful incitement. Johnny Fabre, age 14, is told to do a chore. He's to go out to the woodpile and split logs for the fireplace. For a half-hour he couldn't be more dispirited. Every couple of minutes he hauls off and gives a log a clout. Then all action ceases, as he falls into a reverie.

But all of a sudden, everything changes. Johnny is galvanized into fluid, driving action. His axe makes gleaming silvery semi-circles in the air. The chips fly, log after log is halved then quartered. The pile of firewood rushes upward like a geyser.

You don't have to be a psychologist to guess what's happened. The girl next door, Johnny's best girl at the moment, has appeared in her backyard to take in the clothes. Johnny has an audience—and an incitement to action.

The Importance of Incitement

To make people more effective, to help them produce more and better, requires two things:

a. *Skill and know-how.* This aspect of result-getting is covered in Chapter 12, "Increasing their ability to deliver." You *train* people to improve their abilities in a given area.

b. *Incitement.* This is the urge of the individual to apply his ability to a given objective.

The important thing to remember is this: *You don't have to make a choice* between skill and effort for your mastery of people. Naturally, you want to work on both. However, to improve a person's skill takes time—time for the person to act on your training and make it a part of himself.

But when you step up a man's will to work, you get him to use his *present* skill to better effect. The crucial fact is this: when your incitement is successful, *you get results instantaneously!*

Their unused resources

Nothing comes from nothing. Where does the extra effort come from? How can a person whose will to work has been aroused produce so much more? It's important for you to know the answer, to increase your understanding of incitement.

A number of supervisors and foremen—front-line managers who are in a position to know—were asked these questions:

"How much unused ability do you estimate your people have? How much room for improvement and effort do you feel exists?"

Most of the managers figured their people could do *fully 50% better.* Without increasing a man's ability, they said, the average person could be *twice* as effective *if he wanted to!*

In other words, the average individual has within him a latent capacity that, for the most part, is locked up, is inaccessible *even to himself!* Both he and you break into the treasurehouse of stored effort when you are successful in inciting him to action.

Question: "Why can't a man do this for himself?"

Answer: "Few people are in a position to motivate themselves. That's why you often find a man confiding in a boss or superior: "If you hadn't put me up to it, I never could have accomplished that job. *You made me give more than I knew I had!*"

To give more than they know they have—that is the great fulfillment that your mastery of the techniques of incitement can help others achieve.

Meanwhile, back at the powerhouse

Engineers have been getting increased efficiency out of equipment in somewhat the same way as successful masters of people have been doing with individuals. The parallel can be illuminating:

Over the years, engineers have learned to cut down on the amount of coal needed to make a kilowatt hour of electricity. Several decades ago, it took three pounds of coal to yield a kilowatt hour. Today, it takes about one. Did it take radical changes in equipment? No. The engineers did it without redesigning the boilers; they just followed a policy of "tightening up" in various elements of the equipment.

In the same way, you don't have to wait around for a better breed of human being. By learning the techniques of incitement, you'll get better performance—far better performance—than even the individual himself knew he was capable of.

The carrot and the stick

In general, people can be pushed to achieve by two basic motivators:

. . . *the carrot.* The person is induced to greater effort by rewards of one kind or another.

. . . *the stick.* The person is pushed to greater effort by threats, the possibility or fact of punishment.

However, note that these two figures of speech were developed in the context of getting a *mule* to act. As the old fable has it, you can make the mule move along the road by dangling a carrot before him, or by beating him with a stick.

These two approaches tell the story for getting animals to perform.

When the problem moves up the ladder of the animal kingdom to man, the procedure, as you know, becomes less simple.

The three levels of incitement

To understand what happens when you bring the techniques of incitement into play on human beings, begin by realizing that there are *three* levels of incitement.

It was a teacher of philosophy, Professor Henry Magid, of New York City College, who first suggested to me the three-level nature of incitement. He put it in terms of student accomplishment. Here's how Professor Magid put the idea, leaving the factor of native capacity aside:

A C student: studies because his parents have told him he must.

A B student: studies because he agrees that it's desirable.

An A student: studies because *he* wants to, *he's* interested in the subject, *he* wants to score at college, and so on.

Remember, a few pages back, the point was made that few people are capable of motivating themselves? Yet, it is the expert inciter who eventually achieves exactly this result: he has been so successful in his incitement that the other person *internalizes* the drive. The impulse to perform comes *not* from the outside—for example, because someone tells him to—but from the inside because he himself wants to!

President Eisenhower was very much aware of this secret. That's why he described the effective master of people as the man who could, ". . . make a man do something you want done because he wants to do it."

The secret of incitement

One unexpected thing about incitement: you can state its basic principle in a brief sentence. Even better—you can do it in a word! The cardinal rule of incitement is this:

Make the person goal-minded.

It's that simple. *Goal-mindedness* lies at the heart of every instance of successful incitement.

Now that you know the principle, we'll go on to the four steps by which you apply it to individuals, to mobilize their latent powers with results that, in some cases, can be dazzling!

Dazzling? You may say, "Isn't that laying it on with a trowel?"

Definitely not! Cases like these are commonplace: A failing student, properly incited, can become honors-list material; a shiftless, ne'er-do-well can become a serious, industrious worker; a bored, directionless man or woman can become an interested and interesting expert in a specialized field of study or endeavor; a poor employee can be made a good one, a good employee can be made outstanding.

Transformations like the above are all possible, when, as a master of people, you incite successfully.

Remember, we said the key was *goal-mindedness*. Here are the four steps that can lead you to near-magical results like the instances mentioned above:

1. Make the goal specific

One of the saddest, most pitiable human beings you can come across is the person who has "nowhere to go." You find him stuck in a job or in a social rut or simply in a deadend of living.

Robert L. Simmonds, my ex-boss at the Celanese plant in Newark, and one of the most capable and likeable men I've ever met, told me this incident:

"We had a young foreman here, in his thirties, who had been a foreman for years. He was in charge of one of our smaller departments and wasn't likely to ever budge out of that spot. I felt he was cut out for better things, but he never gave a sign of it. One morning we got to talking and I said, 'Bud, you've been head of the Chopout Room for the past eight years. Wouldn't you like a change?'

" 'I sure would,' he said, 'but I don't know how to go about it.'

" 'No one's going to hand you anything on a silver platter,' I told him. 'You've got to deserve a promotion before you get one.'

" 'Just tell me what to do,' he asked. Usually, I never go along with that kind of request, but I made an exception in Bud's case. 'Go to night school,' I told him, 'study blueprint reading, for a starter.'

"All he needed was a push. He took the blueprint reading, went on to study drafting. Today he's assistant head of Engineering down at one of our southern plants."

What Bob Simmonds had done for Bud was to give him a clear-cut, specific goal to shoot at. Cutting through the fog, the vagueness that surrounds so many people, giving them a sharply-defined, recognizable objective—that's the first step for getting action.

For one person it may be suggesting a course to study. For another it might be a lead to a job opportunity. For a third, it may be not so much your telling him, but guiding a discussion in which you help him clarify *for himself* what he *really* wants to do.

"Life's so dull," a friend once said, "I don't know what to do with myself."

The question was tossed back to him: "What kind of activity would you really, deeply enjoy?"

The answer—which he eventually supplied for himself—was to join a local historical society. He had always been interested in the community's roots in the past. His participation in the society's activities has added great interest and satisfaction to his life—and made him a much-sought-after expert in the history of his town.

In many cases, by clarifying the basic goal of a person's activity, you completely change his attitude towards it. Look at the change some unknown genius at IBM wrought by clarifying a goal *simply by a change in a job title*:

IBM's employees who service typewriters aren't called *typewriter mechanics*. Call them that and they and their superiors get mad. They're referred to as "customer engineers." What's in a name, you ask? Plenty. The men have a much clearer idea of what they're supposed to be doing—and it's *not* repairing typewriters—it's rendering service to the customer! Does it change their attitude and their behavior? You bet!

The chief administrator of an architectural firm recently helped a new receptionist find more interest in her job and perform it very much better. He incited her by this one sentence:

"Sitting at that reception desk, Helen, you get to talk to the most important people in the world—our customers!"

Anything you do to help people see an objective more clearly, to understand what they're supposed to be moving toward, will impel them towards it more directly and with greater dispatch.

2. Make the goal exciting!

This second step adds extra steam for the person who may not quite take off after the first step. He may see a goal, but he may lack the imagination to see it in relation to himself.

"O.K., so I study blueprint reading," Bob Simmonds' Bud might have said to himself.

You make the goal exciting and attractive by spelling out for the other person *what's in it for him:*

"Nancy, if you add shorthand to your typing skills, you'll be able to command a salary 25% higher than you're making now. And not only that, but you'll qualify for much more interesting jobs."

Want to see the papers fly? Tell a file clerk: "You can leave as soon as you get that batch of letters finished."

The incitement here grows out of the *personal gain* the individual sees in his activity.

There are two kinds of rewards or benefits you can stress for people:

. . . *material benefits.* "Tom," the boss says, "you qualify for the higher hourly rate if you keep turning out the quality and quantity of work you've been producing lately." Will Tom redouble his efforts to make the higher grade? Obviously.

Material benefits may be cash, a higher salary rate, privileges. One incitement-wise mother gets results by telling her daughter: "Vicki, if you do a careful and consistent job of helping me around the house, between now and Easter, I'll help you buy that party dress and shoes you've wanted."

. . . *"psychic" rewards.* There are many benefits a man may win that are essentially emotional. Sales managers, for example, have discovered that a top salesman, who'd yawn at a contest to win a cash prize, will turn himself into a pretzel, and sell his head off to become a "regional advisor" or to gain some other status title.

Surprising? No. The sage who said, "We live not by bread alone," said a mouthful.

Here's another situation in which your mastery of people can be decidedly advanced by praise. Not that praise in itself is an effective inciter, but it creates two by-products, either one of which, for certain people, will get them leaping for the moon:

a. *Self-satisfaction.* When you praise a man, honestly and deservedly, you're boosting his self-esteem. One of the greatest satisfactions in this world—or any other that we know of right now—comes to the man who is pleased with himself.

b. *Respect of others.* Public acknowledgment of a man's worth lets everyone in on a secret no one wants kept—least of all the man involved —that he's scored a noteworthy success. The "for he's a jolly good fellow" tune is sweet music to anybody's ears.

You incite people, in short, when you tell them of the pot of gold at the end of the rainbow—the things they'll gain by their superior effort.

3. Increase the goal's attainability

"Boss, I'll never be able to check accounts at the same rate the other girls do . . ."

Many a person has become de-motivated by the seeming hopelessness of a goal. You can often turn the tide by cutting the obstacles down to size.

For example, if Mary's boss were a real hep executive, he might say: "I've been studying your work, and I find that while the others do an average of about 25, you do 20. Twenty's not too bad, and your work is extremely accurate, which is all to the good. Now, I'm sure you can beat that 20 figure. Do it this way. Instead of trying to make the leap from 20 to 25, let's say in the next few days you try to hit 21. Does that seem possible?"

"Sure," says Mary. "Shouldn't have any trouble doing one more."

Mary reaches the 21 figure. A few days later, she gets to 22. See how it goes?

Analyze the approach that Mary's boss used, and you see the two elements that increase a goal's attainability:

. . . *encouragement,* warm avowal that you know the person is capable of performing up to the desired level. You've seen it happen too often yourself to doubt it. The person who *knows* he can do something has a thousand-times better chance of achieving it than the one who hangs back in doubt. And where he is doubtful, your encouragement replaces the doubt by a good dose of self-confidence.

. . . *sub-goals.* Psychologists have long known that breaking a job into parts makes it seem less forbidding, more easily reached. Mary's boss used sub-goals when he broke down the five-account differential that existed between Mary's count and the group average. "Do 21 first. That's easy, isn't it, to do just one more . . ."

By helping people see a given job in terms of sub-goals, you rob a given task of much of its terror or discouragement. You can set sub-goals in terms of:

Time. A yearly quota may seem overwhelming, but exactly the same goal divided by 52 seems perfectly attainable.

Distance. "We've covered five miles," says the scout leader, lessening the weariness of a ten-mile hike, "only five more to go."

Workload. "If we handle 20 drums an hour," the warehousing head tells his men, "we'll get the whole room cleared by the end of the week."

Any time you can slice a goal down to size, subdivide it into digestible, bite-size pieces, you stimulate a man to work with a will, because he feels more certain he can deliver what's needed.

4. Raise his sights—permanently

As a master of people, you'll find that the first three steps will incite people to give that extra effort that can make the difference between an also-ran and a winner. Further, as a master of people, you don't want to be content with a temporary result. This is especially true if the people you're working with have more than a passing relationship with you—they may be your employees or members of your family or lodge brothers.

Your incitement of people needn't be a one-shot affair. You can make *permanent* changes in the lives of people's efforts.

One of the factors you have to fight is a simple psychological fact: interest and motivation tend to sag. People can't play over their heads all the time.

To help people make the improvement in performance permanent, remind them that they're in a position to do it: "You're in the big time now," an executive tells his assistant who has just turned in an outstanding report. "With this under your belt, you've got no place to go but up . . ."

Remind the individual that he's performed up to a higher set of standards—and there's no reason for backsliding.

Usually, there's no problem. Once a man has his wind up, and tastes the fruits of success, his appetite increases for more of the same. It may be up to you simply to help him reset his new goals:

"That was a great talk," the president of a small town newspaper tells one of his reporters, who has just addressed a woman's group on the policies of the newspaper. "I'm going to see to it that you get signed up for more appearances. You can do great things for the paper's public relations."

You can't be amitious *for* people. That can be disastrous—as many a heartbroken parent has found out, trying in vain to push a son or daughter towards a goal they don't accept. But you *can* stimulate people's aspirations and ambition—often towards goals that they themselves feel they couldn't attain.

▶ Recap ◀

This chapter has been about one of the miracle tools in your master toolkit. It can make a matchgirl into a queen, or a second-rate secretary into a topnotch one.

Remember that there are three levels to incitement. Strive to achieve the third, most effective level, when the individual takes the bit in his teeth and goes for broke—towards the goal that you set—because *he* wants to achieve it!

Here are the four steps that create goal-mindedness and give you the benefits of incitement:

1. Make his goal specific.
2. Make the goal exciting!
3. Increase the goal's attainability.
4. Raise his sights—permanently.

Apply these steps, and your mastery will gain for you a better performance, and a better man—to both his and your mutual credit and gain.

Part IV

Push for
the Payoff

chapter 17

For 22 years, Patrick Kinsella pushed coins through a New York subway change window. But one day a crisis interrupted the work routine.

A passenger dashed up to break the news: a woman had gotten her foot pinned between a subway car and the platform on the level below.

Kinsella sprang into action. He ordered another employee to call the police emergency squad. Then he slammed his change window shut and dashed down the steps. The scene he witnessed was utter chaos, men and women milling about helplessly. Two men supported the victim between them, trying to take her weight off the pinned leg.

The miracle of leadership

Kinsella took command. He shouted to the passengers to come out of the car. Then he directed everybody to line up alongside the car and place their hands against the unyielding steel side.

three-prong
leadership
— an idea
that has swept
the business
field

Voices protested that it was useless: nothing that heavy could be moved. When they were all in position, Patrick Kinsella shouted, "Push!"

Housewives, stenographers, businessmen, clerks, obeyed the command. Almost imperceptibly the car tilted. That was enough. Several people lifted the woman and her leg came free.

Patrick Kinsella's feat demonstrated some key aspects of leadership:

. . . the *need* for leadership that a crisis creates.

. . . the *ability* of a self-confident, knowledgeable leader to pull off a miracle.

. . . the *obedience* of people to a leader who obviously knows what he's doing.

Needed: leadership

Our daily lives, our most ordinary living situations, are bedeviled by the need for leadership. Consider these examples:

Heartbreak house. A friend of my wife's is a beautiful, charming woman. She's a housewife, but her house is always a mess. She's had a succession of cleaning women; baby sitters and assorted help come and go. "I can't seem to get them to understand what I want done," she says. She's got a leadership problem. It frustrates her otherwise pleasant existence, sours the atmosphere of her home.

Embittered millionaire. Mr. R. T. figures his income in the hundreds of thousands. His operations range from raw cotton and acetate flake to name-brand merchandise. That's a lot of territory even in the textile field. But Mr. T. has a leadership problem: "My associates don't respect me." It embitters every moment of his waking life.

Manager in the red. A plant manager has been struggling to increase the efficiency of his plant. Try as he can, month after month shows him operating at a loss. He can't seem to get the wholehearted cooperation of his people. He's got a leadership problem—and an ulcer.

Parents—all of them—have problems of leadership to wrestle with day in, day out.

So do teachers.

And heads of community and civic organizations.

And officers of clubs and lodges.

And people in management, from supervisors up to the highest levels.

And so does everyone who now guides, or at some later time expects to guide, the activities of others.

"When the king has a bellyache, the people groan," states the old proverb. And it's true enough. One way or another, followers suffer the effects of leader's difficulties.

Consider, for example, the employees—cleaning women, the baby sitters—of the frustrated housewife. They undoubtedly have a rough time of it.

And how about the associates of our textile tycoon? Haven't *they* got a problem? What particular kind of hell do their jobs become, having to work under a leader they dislike?

Have you ever been inside a plant that's operating in the red? You can sense the tension and insecurity in the workers' movements, words, eyes.

The problem of leadership

"Leaders are born, not made." That's been said a thousand times. There's some basis to the idea, or it wouldn't pop up as often as it does. Yet, there's a fallacy to the statement, and here it is:

True, some people seem to have a natural knack for getting the loyalty and cooperation of others. But the reasons that those who *don't* have the knack fail to acquire it is that there are few *systems* of leadership that can be studied and mastered.

Ideas about leadership abound. You've heard many of them:

The drill sergeant idea: "A leader should be an aggressive individual with a loud, commanding voice."

The mirror idea: "A leader is the man who reflects the wishes of the group. When they follow him, they're really following their own ideals."

The trait idea: "A leader must be alert, courageous, flexible, honest," etc., etc. This approach suggests that the leader is the man with a particular mix of qualities.

The personality idea: "The leader has an X element in his personal make-up that is somehow detected by others, that attracts them, and wins their loyalty."

Note that not one of these ideas suggests a *systematic* approach to leadership. They all attempt to pin down what a leader has that makes him one. And all these ideas have one fault in common: none can be used by a would-be leader as a clue to becoming a leader or in improving leadership ability. For example, how can one practice being aggressive or developing a loud, commanding voice? How can one practice—with any hope of success—being alert, courageous, etc., etc.?

Found at last—a new system of leadership

This chapter will describe for you a leadership method developed by this author that can be learned easily. It is simple and has won the enthusiastic approval of thousands of people. Here are a few items that give you some idea of how widespread its acceptance has been:

The book in which the idea was originally developed—*How to Be a Successful Leader*—has sold tens of thousands of copies, and has been translated into German, Japanese and Portuguese. Ten years after first publication, it has been reprinted in paperback form under the title, *Techniques of Leadership*.

It has been used by psychologists at Boston University in a course in family relations; by the president of a fraternal organization in Brisbane, Australia, to eliminate his personal leadership difficulties; and by thousands of executives and supervisors throughout the United States and Canada, to improve their on-the-job effectiveness.

Give the three-pronged approach to leadership a trial and it will work wonders for you, as it has for thousands of others.

For the moment, forget all the past ideas you may have about leadership. Approach the concept objectively, prepared to apply it, mentally and practically, to real leadership situations. Then judge for yourself how much sense it makes.

The new approach

Until recent years, the belief was widely held that the democratic method of leadership was the most productive one. Leaders who failed to consult with their subordinates were thought not to be "managing" properly. Those who issued "this is the way I want things done" directives were considered relics of the stone age.

Then, in 1953 there appeared the three-way approach that sought to create a more realistic basis for leadership thinking. Taking off on studies made by social psychologist Kurt Lewin, the approach describes three methods of leadership, each having advantages and disadvantages, none holding any claim to being the *one right way*. The three approaches:

1. *Autocratic leadership*—The leader mainly seeks obedience from his group. He determines policy and considers decision-making a one-man operation—and he is the man.

2. *Democratic leadership*—The leader draws ideas and suggestions from the group by discussion and consultation. Group members are encouraged to take part in setting policy. The leader's job is largely that of moderator.

3. *Free-rein leadership*—The leader is more or less an information booth. He plays down his role in the group's activity. He's on hand mainly to provide materials and information. He exercises a minimum of control, his main role being that of setting goals.

As opposed to the old idea that democratic leadership is the one best way, a much broader and more flexible approach is possible, in which *each* of the three methods plays a role.

Lowdown on some old mysteries

Once this new framework has been supplied, some of the contradictions of leadership you've undoubtedly come across can be explained. For example, it becomes clear that you don't have to choose between using *either* the autocratic, democratic, or free-rein method. Forcing such a choice would be like telling a golf player he must choose between using a driver and a putter. *In the course of a game, he'll use both.*

Take a look at Mr. X, an executive who does an outstanding job of leading his people:

He *directs* his secretary to write up a report based on quality-control figures of the last month.

He *consults* with his five department heads on the best way to push a special order through their departments with a minimum of upset to regular production.

He *suggests* to his assistant that it would be a good idea to figure out ways in which they can handle special experimental projects in the future.

Note the different approaches that Executive X uses: he *directs* (autocratic) on one phase of a problem; he *consults* (democratic method) on another phase; he *suggests* an objective (free-rein method) in the third situation.

The skill of leadership lies largely in knowing *when* to use which method, to learn *to vary* techniques to fit the changing conditions and people involved. Get this one point, and you make a major advance in your leadership knowhow.

Let's go on to cover some of the practical aspects of the idea:

Your guide lines

A leader frequently deals with his group individually, on a face-to-face basis. In adjusting your approach to the individual, many factors influence your choice:

• *Age:* A mature person will function better under free-rein leadership; a youngster would probably fare better under the autocratic approach.

• *Sex:* Feminists to the contrary, women generally take to the autocratic approach, whereas, everything else being equal, the democratic or free-rein method works better with men.

• *Training and experience:* The more familiar a subordinate is with his job or assignment, the more the democratic or free-rein method should be favored.

However, the single most important factor is likely to be personality. And here the recent work of social psychologists can be of direct help.

A group of psychologists—T. W. Adorno, Else Frenkel-Brunswik, D. J. Levinson, and R. N. Sanford—have theorized that there is a type of individual with a definite emotional predisposition toward autocratic leadership. They pooled their findings in a book entitled "The Authoritarian Personality."

Here is a thumbnail description of several personality types, based on this unusual study:

1. *The "authoritarian" personality*—His own town, country, lan-

guage, he feels, are best. He tends to be provincial; economically and politically, he is usually conservative. Conforming to accepted customs is very important to him. He dislikes "weakness"—either in individuals or groups. Therefore, minority groups draw his disapproval in greater or lesser degree. And by the same token, leadership that isn't "strong" seems to him to be weak and undesirable.

2. *The "equalitarian" personality*—Psychologists who have studied the authoritarian personality likewise speak of the "equalitarian" personality.

This type tends to be liberal-minded about most things—whether it's politics or the table manners his neighbor displays. Generally, he feels that people should be judged on individual merits, rather than on the basis of their religion, nationality, or the degree to which they conform to prevailing customs. To him, the autocratic leader may seem to be dictatorial and undesirable; democratic leadership and democratic processes are most admired.

3. *The "libertarian" personality*—The scientists haven't obliged with a description of a personality type with the emotional predisposition to free-rein leadership. But it's possible, by extrapolation, to describe the type in general. He tends to be somewhat of an introvert. He likes to be on his own, is self-confident, feels capable of working out means if he's told the ends. Often he has a technical mind and is likely to be highly skilled in his job. Usually, he is attracted to jobs that require precision or an intellectual approach. He's likely to think of direction from a superior as "control" and interference.

Simplifying the personality factor

Fortunately, you don't have to take a psychoanalyst's view of people, or brush up on a comprehensive theory of personality in evaluating individuals. A rule-of-thumb method for sizing up individuals can give you the clues you need. Below are some examples.

With these, be autocratic:

The hostile person. He resents authority but respects it at the same time. Accordingly, his hostility must be met by a show of authority. The autocratic approach has the effect of channeling his aggressiveness, confining his energies to constructive ends.

The dependent person. This type feels the need for firm rule. His sense of dependence gives him a feeling of being at loose ends, up in the air unless the leader is authoritative and dominant. Firm guidance gives him reassurance.

The cooperative person. An individual who is cooperative is not necessarily unaggressive. But his aggressiveness, unlike that of hostile individuals, takes constructive paths. The cooperative-aggressive individual will work best with democratic control.

The group-minded individual. The man who enjoys "team play" will probably function best if your approach to him is democratic. He needs less direction, since he regards work as a group job.

With these, use the free-rein approach:

The individualist, the solo player. He is usually most productive under the free-rein type of leadership if he knows his job. Even if he tends to be a show-off, a "grandstand player," let him have his head, unless considerations of group welfare, or resentment of other individuals force you to modify your approach.

The social isolationist. Whether you call them introverts or describe them as "withdrawn," some people have an aversion to interpersonal contact. Whatever the cause may be, such individuals are likely to do their best work on their own. The atmosphere created by the free-rein approach is most conducive to their peace of mind and most effective efforts.

When the situation provides your cue

The situation in which you operate is another factor that guides your choice of method. For example:

A fire breaks out in a plant. The department head, regardless of his usual leadership methods, is likely to handle the situation with a series of orders to those around him—the autocratic method. Clearly, disaster conditions demand immediate obedience to orders; anything else might lead to catastrophe. In any situation calling for fast, decisive action, the autocratic approach is a natural one.

Or, take the case of the head of a quality-control unit who has had much success leading his group by democratic discussion methods. Then he has a disagreement with one of his assistants, and soon finds his group divided into two opposing camps. As a consequence of this factionalism, it becomes impossible to achieve results in group meetings.

The group leader finally resolved his problem by changing from a democratic to an autocratic approach. He made his views clear to the group, explained the reasons for adopting these views, and as a final step, stated that his views would be the ones followed.

In this example, the democratic approach was no longer effective amid the mutual hostility dividing the group. Instead, the autocratic method was the approach that held most promise of success.

Goals as your guide

Finally, it's what you want of the group that often determines your choice of method. For example:

1. *Compliance*—The leader whose group is working along routine lines, with well-established and easily achieved goals, will find the autocratic approach especially appropriate. The assumption here is that group goals are best met by merely following instructions.

2. *Cooperation*—An unusual work order puts pressure on the group to perform above standards. It may mean working longer hours, increasing effort or work pace. Calling the group together, describing the nature of the situation, asking for help and suggestions for meeting the needs of the moment, are democratic procedures that will help meet objectives.

3. *Creativity*—Productivity can be stimulated slightly by autocratic means, considerably by democratic approaches. But *creativity* poses different demands. Where novel ideas are required, where imagination is looked for, the free-rein approach is usually the most effective. The free-rein leader who explains the problem or the need, and encourages group members on an individual basis, is most likely to spark the imagination of the people working under him.

Test your leadership and followership

The three-pronged approach to leadership has been used as a basis for developing two tests—one for leadership tendencies of individuals, the second for their "followership" tendencies. Followership means the type of leadership under which an individual *prefers to work*. Generally, it's the type under which he will be most productive and will achieve the greatest satisfaction.

You'll find both tests below.

Test yourself

The questions below will indicate the *type of leader you tend to be* and the *type of leadership you prefer to work under.* Some of the questions you will be able to answer off-hand. Others may require careful thought. But answer all questions as accurately and honestly as possible. When a question has no direct bearing to your experience, indicate what you believe you would do or think in the situation described. The scoring will be found following the tests.

Leadership Tendencies

	YES	NO
1. Do you enjoy "running the show"?	( )	( )
2. Generally, do you think it's worth the effort to explain to subordinates the reasons for a decision or policy before putting it into effect?	( )	( )
3. Do you prefer the administrative end of your leadership job—planning, paperwork, etc.—to supervising or working with your subordinates?	( )	( )
4. A stranger comes into your department and you know he's the new employee hired by one of your assistants. On approaching him, would you first ask his name rather than introduce yourself?	( )	( )
5. Do you keep your people up-to-date on developments affecting them?	( )	( )
6. In giving out assignments, do you tend to state the goals, leave methods to your subordinates?	( )	( )
7. Do you think that it's good common sense for a leader to keep aloof from his people, because in the long run familiarity breeds lessened respect?	( )	( )
8. Comes time to decide about a group outing. The majority prefer to have it on Wednesday, but you're pretty sure Thursday is better for all concerned. Would you put the question to a vote rather than make the decision yourself?	( )	( )

Leadership Tendencies

	YES	NO
9. If you had your way, would you make running your group a push-button affair, with personal contacts and communications held to a minimum?	( )	( )
10. Do you find it fairly easy to fire someone?	( )	( )
11. The friendlier you are with your people, the better you can lead them. Correct?	( )	( )
12. After considerable time, you dope out the answer to a work problem. Your assistant promptly pokes it full of holes. Would you be annoyed that the problem is still unsolved, rather than become angry with the assistant?	( )	( )
13. Do you agree that one of the best ways to avoid problems of discipline is to provide adequate punishments for violations of rules?	( )	( )
14. Your way of handling a situation is being criticized. Would you try to sell your viewpoint rather than state that, as boss, your word is final?	( )	( )
15. Do you generally leave it up to your subordinates to contact you, as far as informal day-to-day communications are concerned?	( )	( )
16. Do you expect subordinates to feel personally loyal to you?	( )	( )
17. Do you favor the practice of appointing a committee to settle a problem rather than stepping in to decide on it yourself?	( )	( )
18. Some experts say differences of opinion within a group are healthy. Agree?	( )	( )

Followership Tendencies

	YES	NO
1. When given an assignment, do you like to have all details spelled out?	( )	( )
2. Do you think that, by and large, bosses are bossier than they need be?	( )	( )

Followership Tendencies

	YES	NO
3. Would you say that initiative is one of your strong points?	( )	( )
4. Do you feel a boss lowers himself by mingling socially with his subordinates?	( )	( )
5. In general, would you prefer working with others to working alone?	( )	( )
6. Do you prefer the pleasures of solitude (reading, listening to music) to the social pleasures of being with others (parties, get-togethers, etc.)?	( )	( )
7. Do you tend to become strongly attached to the bosses you work under?	( )	( )
8. Do you tend to offer a helping hand to the newcomers among your colleagues and fellow workers?	( )	( )
9. Do you enjoy using your own ideas and ingenuity to solve a work problem?	( )	( )
10. Do you prefer the kind of boss who knows all the answers, to one who, not infrequently, comes to you for help?	( )	( )
11. Do you feel it's OK for your boss to be friendlier with some members of the group than with others?	( )	( )
12. Do you like to assume full responsibility for assignments, rather than just do the work and leave the responsibility to your boss?	( )	( )
13. Do you feel that "mixed" groups—men working with women, for example—naturally tend to have more friction than unmixed ones?	( )	( )
14. If you learned your boss was having an affair with his secretary, would your respect for him remain undiminished?	( )	( )
15. Have you often felt that "he travels fastest who travels alone"?	( )	( )

Followership Tendencies

	YES	NO
16. Would you agree: a boss who can't win your loyalty shouldn't be boss?	( )	( )
17. Would you get upset by a fellow worker whose inability or ineptitude obstructs the work or your group?	( )	( )
18. Do you think "boss" is a dirty word?	( )	( )

Leadership Scoring Key

To get your score, follow this procedure for each test:

a. Ring all the question-numbers below to which you answered "Yes."

Leadership	Followership
I. 1, 4, 7, 10, 13, 16	I. 1, 4, 7, 10, 13, 16
II. 2, 5, 8, 11, 14, 17	II. 2, 5, 8, 11, 14, 17
III. 3, 6, 9, 12, 15, 18	III. 3, 6, 9, 12, 15, 18

b. Count the "Yes" answers you've indicated for rows I, II and III and fill in the three totals in the columns below.

Leadership	Followership
I. Autocratic _____	I. Autocratic _____
II. Democratic _____	II. Democratic _____
III. Free-rein _____	III. Free-rein _____

Interpreting the results

The following analysis applies to both your leadership and followership scores. In general, there are three possible scoring trends that might be recorded.

High scores. Any category in which you scored from 4 to 6 "yes" answers is one toward which your inclinations are strong. Let's say, for instance, that your leadership score read like this: autocratic-5; democratic-3; free-rein-1. Your autocratic leadership tendencies would be quite pronounced.

Or take this possible followership score: autocratic-0; democratic-6; free-rein-1. It's a safe bet that a person getting this kind of score has a strong preference for democratic leadership. In addition, he has tendencies *away from* the other two types.

Low scores. Another possibility is that your score didn't go above three "yes" answers in any of the categories. Here's a followership score of this kind: autocratic-2; democratic-2; free-rein-1.

Low scores indicate an individual without strong feelings about working under any of the three types of leadership. He would do almost as well under a boss using any one of the three methods.

Balanced scores. A particularly interesting type of score is one of this kind: autocratic-3; democratic-3; free-rein-3.

Evenly distributed scores generally reveal a personality sympathetic to all three methods. People who make this kind of score have a well-proportioned personality. It's a desirable balance. Under ordinary circumstances, they will have less of a problem in adjusting to any superior-subordinate relationship.

Such a score, however, is not usual. The reason is that preference for the autocratic and free-rein methods often requires emotional outlooks that are directly opposed to one another. Such conflicting elements seldom are found within a single individual.

In most cases, balance is less perfect. Let's say your scores were slightly off balance—3, 2, 1, for example. Your autocratic preference is there all right, but it's not too pronounced. Chances are, people with these scores would find as little difficulty in working under a free-rein leader than an autocratic one.

▶ Recap ◀

This chapter has described a tradition-busting approach to leadership. Up until about ten years ago, most human relations authorities were pushing the virtues of democratic leadership above all others: "Give people a chance to participate in discussions about their activities. Give them a voice in making decisions and you'll get the best possible follow-through."

The three-pronged approach doesn't knock democratic leadership, but it *does* put it in perspective. It is pointed out that two other types of leadership—autocratic and free-rein—also have their perfectly good place in your day-to-day leadership activity. Briefly, here's what the three leadership types come down to—

. . . *autocratic* leadership. You're the boss. Mainly, you ask obedience from your group.

. . . *democratic* leadership. You let others in on discussions about policies and decisions. Here your leadership role is largely that of moderator.

. . . *free-rein* leadership. You let each individual more or less have his head. You play down your leadership role, act more or less as a guide and information booth.

Several factors determine which of the three methods you use in a given situation:

The nature of the individual or individuals you're dealing with, their age, sex, training and so on. As far as the personality factor is concerned:

You use the *autocratic* approach with the *hostile* person and the *dependent* person.

You use the *democratic* approach with the *cooperative* and *group-minded* individual.

You use the *free-rein* approach with the *individualist* and the *social isolationist.*

In using goals as your guide:

. . . when you want *compliance* use the autocratic technique.

. . . when you want *cooperation* use the democratic technique.

. . . when you want *creativity*—novel ideas, imagination—use the free-rein technique.

Finally, to get an insight into your own leadership and follower-ship tendencies, take the self-rating tests starting on page 226 and apply this knowledge to help you still further increase your leadership effectiveness.

chapter 18

Now we come to the last lap, the last chapter of this book. Before writing this chapter, I asked myself a tough question: "What is the single most helpful idea I can put into the closing chapter? What idea or concept can I use for a finale that will wrap up everything put into the preceding chapters, give the reader a closing thought that will make it possible for him to put down this book and say, 'I've gotten my money's worth. I'll be able to put every suggestion and recommendation to work. I'm sure I'll succeed in the mastery of the tools provided.'"

The cause of success

I think you'll agree that's a pretty tough objective I set myself. But I'm also sure you'll agree when you conclude this chapter *that I was successful!* The concept of the slight edge does give you the angle you need to galvanize

the sharp
edge
of success

yourself into action, to push ahead with your aspirations to leadership, to the mastery and management of people.

Read, and reap!

The principle of the slight edge was first expounded to me by Professor Aaron Levenstein of New York City College many years ago. At first it remained merely an idea, interesting, intriguing but without any immediate practical value.

As time passed, however, I observed on the business scene, and in the lives of dozens of successful people, the direct application of the principle. For example:

Several years ago I interviewed John H. Mitchell, vice-president in charge of national sales of Screen Gems, Inc., a television production company which shot from $100,000 to a multi-million dollar operation in its first four years.

John Mitchell's name, naturally, is linked closely with the success of Screen Gems in that tough, competitive industry.

I asked the question without which such a discussion is never complete: "Mr. Mitchell, how do you explain your phenomenal advancement in the television film business?"

He smiled. "I was just a little better than the other fellow."

Boastful? That's what I thought then. But now, several years later, I understand what John Mitchell was getting at. *He meant what he had said literally*, and he said it well.

In a few simple words, he had stated a formula that almost everyone can apply—the principle of the slight edge. You can use it to build your effectiveness as a leader, as a master and manager of people, indeed, your success in almost any area of accomplishment.

It's this principle of the slight edge that explains the achievement of an executive like Mr. Mitchell and gives you a framework around which you can build a program for the mastery of the tools described in the preceding chapters.

Here's how you can put the idea to work for you.

The principle at work

Let's get back now to the statement of John H. Mitchell: "I was just a little better than the other fellow."

Scientists who have studied individual differences, the variations among pepole, have come up with a startling fact. Here it is, as stated by Dr. David Wechsler in his fascinating book, *The Range of Human Capacities:*

". . . Human variability," says Dr. Wechsler, "when compared to that of other phenomena in nature, is extremely limited, and . . . the differences which separate human beings from one another with respect to whatever trait or ability we may wish to compare, *are far smaller than is ordinarily supposed*" (italics added).

Dr. Wechsler backs up his statement with statistics. He compares the general intelligence of the highest and lowest individuals in a group of about 1,000. How much "smarter" would you guess the high man would be compared to the low? Five times? Ten? No, the answer, *even in this extreme case,* was approximately *two-and-a-half times.*

Dr. Wechsler's figures depend on a comparison of extremes. In everyday life, individuals are more nearly matched. Again, remember the statement: "I was just a little better than the other fellow."

A *slight edge.* That's the secret that explains the individual who makes the grade. In practical terms, you see the principle in operation every day. There's a promotion available in the ABC department. Employees X, Y, and Z are in line for the spot. In the average case, its X, the man who's *just a little better* than either of his colleagues, who gets the promotion.

Once you're aware of the principle, you see proof of it everywhere you turn:

The sports page of *The New York Times* ran a photograph of the finish of the second race at Jamaica recently. Four jockeys are straining over the outstretched necks of racing thoroughbreds. It was a photo finish. The winner, paying $24.10, claimed victory not by lengths or furlongs, *but by a scant inch.* The photograph clearly shows he had the merest shade of advantage at the finish line. *But that's all that was needed to win.*

Or ask the sales manager who works with the head of the production department for days and nights to shave costs a few pennies. He knows that once he's got that *slight edge* in price over his competition, he's in.

William Zeckendorf, president, brain and powerhouse of Webb & Knapp, outstanding real estate firm, expressed the slight edge principle when asked how his organization would stand up under the pressure of changing times: "We'll always be a little better off than the rest of them. We can accelerate a flood tide a little better, and we can resist an ebb tide a little better. That's the difference between the men and the boys in this business."

The slight edge can cut deeply in your favor. Victory can depend on the smallest of improvements. For example, your better understanding of your people makes it possible to assign them to tasks they really go for. Result: better teamwork, skyrocketing achievement.

Or, by successfully motivating your people to give that little extra effort, you achieve the group goal that you've set for them.

Cause and effect

An interesting question arises: why does the principle of the slight edge play so small a part in plans for self-improvement and advancement?

The answer is, for the most part, that we confuse cause and effect. We observe an effective individual in action, for example. He seems so far superior to the average, we conclude that major causes, *large* differences must necessarily account for his achievement.

But look: A man who's 5 foot 6 inches is considered decidedly short. A man 6 feet tall is considered tall. Yet, stand them back to back and heel to heel and there's only a 9% *difference between them.*

Note: The actual difference is very small. But the *result* of that slight edge can be tremendous. It can make the difference between shortness and tallness in one case, an adequate performance and an outstanding one in another.

And therefore, the key executive of a successful business organization can sum up the secret of his effectiveness in the words, "I was just a little better than the other fellow."

The principle of the slight edge works in many ways. In its simplest forms, it tells us we don't have to be twice as good as a competitor, but *only slightly superior* to win out. In almost every game ever devised, the victory goes to the man who scores merely one point or unit more than the opposition. In every contest that is essentially a race towards a goal—swimming, running, sailboating—reaching the finish line a few inches ahead of the field gives you the big win just as certainly as beating the opposition by a mile.

Further applications

There is another, and entirely different way in which the slight edge principle can operate in your favor. In this application, you develop a slight edge, not in the main area of skill, but in a *related* one.

In my own career, it's been this application of the principle that has been extremely helpful. Just consider. My original stock in trade, the qualification I had for starting in the management field, was a first-hand knowledge of management. I had owned and operated a molding shop of my own for a couple of years, learned about the world of business the hard way. I had been a production foreman for the Celanese Corporation of America for seven years, and it was through these years, particularly, that I gained valuable understanding of the problems and processes of management, of the endless complications of human relationships that occur on the job scene.

However, the additional skill I had—and I assure you that it was modest at best—was the ability to express myself in writing. Accordingly, it was the combination of the management skill or knowledge, plus the writing skill that gave me the slight edge needed to establish myself in a difficult and competitive field.

One of the most successful men I know is a lawyer on the legal staff of one of our big oil companies. Is it his tremendous grasp of the law that's put him out front? Obviously, he's no slouch in matters of the law. But it's his knowledge of Spanish that has put him where he is. His company has many dealings with Latin America, and his combination of legal training and his language skill gave him the edge he needed to put him way ahead of the field.

Two points to remember

In order to realize the full significance and promise of the slight edge principle, there are two points to keep in mind:

. . . *it's self-feeding.* Like the atomic "breeder" reaction, once you have a little to start with, you have a self-generating process on your hands. What happens in practice is that one forward step puts you in a position to take another. And another. And another. In each situation, the principle of the slight edge operates, waiting to be used, capitalized on.

In most cases, you'll find the highly effective and successful individual has achieved his position by a series of *small* upward steps. "Success is a fruit of slow growth," wrote the English novelist, Henry Fielding.

Exceptions? Of course. You'll find the occasional man who has rocketed straight to the top. But he's the long shot. You don't have to count on odds of that order to help you win.

. . . *it gives you a realistic goal.* Social psychologist Kurt Lewin, in *Resolving Social Conflicts,* points out: "A successful individual typically sets his next goal somewhat, but not too much, above his last achievement. In this way he steadily raises his level of aspiration. Although in the long run he is guided by his ideal goal, which may be rather high, nevertheless, *his real goal for the next step is kept realistically close to his present position*" (italics added).

Remember? "I was just a little better than the other fellow."

This process of being a little better is the means by which you set your short-range goals, and eventually achieve your long-range objectives. In other words, the slight edge principle can pinpoint the moves leading to the application of the human relations tools described in each of the previous chapters. Put them to work *now*—knowing your goal is not dreamy fantasy, but hard-headed reality. You're not out to beat the world but to achieve a *slight edge.*

And then, you make that wonderful discovery all over again—that by achieving the slight edge, *you have indeed become a world-beater!*

▶ Recap ◀

You don't need a recapitulation for this chapter. Like a sun tan, re-expose yourself every once in a while, when you see you're in need of a little refresher. It makes great reading, even better doing.